THE CHILD'S WORLD®

Encyclopedia of the
NFL

VOLUME FOUR: Super Bowl XIII >> Zone Blitz

By James Buckley, Jr.

Jim Gigliotti

Matt Marini

John Wiebusch

KEY TO SYMBOLS

Throughout *The Child's World® Encyclopedia of the NFL*, you'll see these symbols. They'll give you a quick clue pointing to each entry's subject.

| *Active Coach* | *Active Player* | *Football Term* | *Hall of Fame* | *Miscellaneous* | *Stadium* | *Super Bowl* | *Team* |

The Child's World
www.childsworld.com

Published in the United States of America by The Child's World®
1980 Lookout Drive, Mankato, MN 56003-1705
800-599-READ • www.childsworld.com

ACKNOWLEDGMENTS

The Child's World®: Mary Berendes, Publishing Director

Produced by Shoreline Publishing Group LLC
President / Editorial Director: James Buckley, Jr.
Designer: Tom Carling, carlingdesign.com
Assistant Editors: Jim Gigliotti, Matt Marini

Interior Photo Credits:
AP/Wide World: 6, 9, 11, 23, 24, 27, 29, 41, 44, 45, 48, 53, 54, 64, 75, 79, 81, 91, 94, 97, 103;
Corbis: 66, 98; Getty Images: 18, 20. All other images provided by Focus on Football.
Icons created by Robert Pizzo.

LIBRARY OF CONGRESS CATALOG-IN-PUBLICATION DATA

The Child's World encyclopedia of the NFL / by James Buckley, Jr. ... [et al.].
    p. cm.
Includes index.
ISBN 978-1-59296-922-7 (v. 1 : alk. paper) – ISBN 978-1-59296-923-4 (v. 2 : alk. paper)
– ISBN 978-1-59296-924-1 (v. 3 : alk. paper) – ISBN 978-1-59296-925-8 (v. 4 : alk. paper)
1. National Football League–Encyclopedias, Juvenile. 2. Football–United States–Encyclopedias, Juvenile.
I. Buckley, James, 1963– II. Child's World (Firm) III. Title: Encyclopedia of the NFL.
    GV955.5.N35C55 2007
    796.332'64--dc22
                  2007005662

■ *Doak Walker*

S INCE ITS FOUNDING IN 1920, THE National Football League has played more than 12,000 games in 100 U.S. cities—and 10 countries. More than 17,000 players have strapped on their pads. They've combined to put up more than 400,000 points and score more than 45,000 touchdowns. That, my friends, is an awful lot of football!

In *The Child's World® Encyclopedia of the NFL*, we won't have room to include all of those players or recount all of those touchdowns. But we've put our helmets together and tried to give a complete picture of the very best and most important people, places, teams, and terms that football fans like you want to know more about.

You'll meet great members of the Pro Football Hall of Fame and read about today's top players. You'll relive some of the NFL's most memorable moments—from the Sneaker Game to the Coldest Game to the Greatest Game Ever Played. Need to learn how to "talk football"? These books will help you understand the terms and phrases you'll hear during a game. Finally, each of the NFL's 32 teams is covered with a complete history. All you'll need to enjoy these books is a love of football . . . and a knowledge of the alphabet!

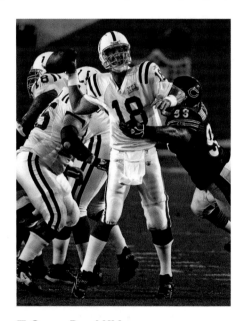

■ *Super Bowl XLI*

Contents: Volume 4: Super Bowl XIII ≫ Zone Blitz

Super Bowl XIII

In the first rematch of Super Bowl opponents, the Steelers got the better of the Cowboys for the second time in four seasons. Pittsburgh also had beaten Dallas in Super Bowl X. This game was an exciting offensive battle that was not decided until Steelers running back Rocky Bleier recovered an onside kick in the final minute of the game.

Pittsburgh became the first franchise to win the Super Bowl three times. Unlike its first two championships earlier in the decade, which were won behind a dominant defense, the club relied on the strong arm of quarterback Terry Bradshaw to win game XIII. Bradshaw passed for 318 yards to earn the MVP award. He completed 17 of his 30 attempts, and threw four touchdown passes.

■ *Bradshaw led the way with four TD passes.*

PITTSBURGH STEELERS 35, DALLAS COWBOYS 31

January 21, 1979

Orange Bowl • Miami, Florida

ATTENDANCE: 79,484

Pittsburgh (AFC)	7	14	0	14 —	35
Dallas (NFC)	7	7	3	14 —	31

MVP: **Terry Bradshaw, QB, Pittsburgh**

HEAD COACHES
PITTSBURGH: **Chuck Noll**
DALLAS: **Tom Landry**

Three of Bradshaw's scoring tosses came in the first half. Two were to wide receiver John Stallworth; the third was to Bleier. The latter was a seven-yard strike that came 26 seconds before the end of the second quarter, giving the Steelers a 21-14 halftime lead.

It was 21-17 before Pittsburgh scored two touchdowns within a span of 19 seconds in the fourth quarter. First, Franco Harris capped an 85-yard drive by rushing 22 yards for a touchdown. Then, the Steelers recovered a fumble on the ensuing kickoff. On the next play, Bradshaw teamed with Lynn Swann on an 18-yard touchdown pass to make it 35-17 with 6:51 to go.

Quarterback Roger Staubach rallied the Cowboys by passing for two touchdowns after that, including a four-yarder to Butch Johnson with 22 seconds left, but it wasn't enough.

Super Bowl XIV

Defending-champion Pittsburgh was a heavy favorite, but the Steelers had to score two touchdowns in the fourth quarter to rally and defeat the pesky Rams. Los Angeles was playing in front of a partisan crowd in Pasadena, California, not far from its home stadium in Los Angeles.

The Rams thrilled that crowd by taking a 19-17 lead in the third quarter. The go-ahead score game on Lawrence McCutcheon's 24-yard, halfback-option pass to wide receiver Ron Smith 4:45 into the period.

Los Angeles' advantage held up until Pittsburgh scored two touchdowns in the fourth quarter. Early in the period, quarterback Terry Bradshaw completed a long pass to wide receiver John Stallworth between two Rams' defenders at the 32-yard line.

Stallworth grabbed the pass and took off to the end zone to finish a 73-yard touchdown play. Later in the quarter, linebacker Jack Lambert thwarted a Los Angeles drive with an interception at the Steelers' 14-yard line. After his 16-yard return to the 30, Pittsburgh embarked on the decisive touchdown drive. Bradshaw's 45-yard pass to Stallworth was the key play, and Franco Harris' one-yard touchdown run put the game out of reach with 1:49 left.

■ *Two in a row for Terry, who holds his MVP trophy.*

Bradshaw finished with 14 completions in 21 attempts for 309 yards and two touchdowns to earn game MVP honors for the second consecutive season. Stallworth had 121 yards on just three catches.

Kick returner Larry Anderson was an unsung star for the Steelers. He gave his team good field position with several long kickoff returns, including runbacks of 45, 38, 37, and 32 yards.

Attendance for the game, held at the world famous Rose Bowl, was 103,985. It remains the largest crowd ever to see an NFL postseason game.

PITTSBURGH STEELERS 31, LOS ANGELES RAMS 19

January 20, 1980

Rose Bowl • Pasadena, California

ATTENDANCE: 103,985

Los Angeles (NFC)	7	6	6	0 —	19
Pittsburgh (AFC)	3	7	7	14 —	31

MVP: **Terry Bradshaw, QB, Pittsburgh**

HEAD COACHES
PITTSBURGH: **Chuck Noll**
LOS ANGELES: **Ray Malavasi**

Super Bowl XV

Veteran quarterback Jim Plunkett, a highly-touted college star whose pro career fizzled in stints with New England and San Francisco, found new life in Super Bowl XV. He earned game MVP honors while leading the Raiders to the victory.

Plunkett completed just 13 passes (in 21 attempts), but they accounted for 261 yards, and three of them went for touchdowns. Cliff Branch was on the receiving end of two of Plunkett's scoring tosses, including a two-yard strike to cap a short touchdown drive the first time that Oakland had the ball. The Raiders got possession at Philadelphia's 30-yard line when linebacker Rod Martin intercepted Eagles quarterback Ron Jaworski on the third play of the game and returned the

■ *In this game, Oakland's No. 16 was No. 1.*

ball 17 yards. It was one of three picks for Martin, setting a Super Bowl record.

Late in the first quarter, with the ball on the Raiders' 20-yard line, Plunkett scrambled away from the Philadelphia pass rush. He lobbed a short pass to running back Kenny King, and King raced 80 yards down the left sideline for a touchdown and a 14-0 lead.

It was 14-3 at halftime, and then the Raiders padded their advantage on the opening possession of the third quarter. Starting from its own 24-yard line, Oakland needed only five plays to cover 76 yards. Plunkett completed a 32-yard pass to Bob Chandler on the third play, then capped the quick drive with a 29-yard touchdown strike to Branch.

The Raiders went on to lead by as many as 21 points (at 24-3) after that.

OAKLAND RAIDERS 27, PHILADELPHIA EAGLES 10

January 25, 1981

Louisiana Superdome
New Orleans, Louisiana

ATTENDANCE: 76,135

Oakland (AFC)	14	0	10	3	— 27
Philadelphia (NFC)	0	3	0	7	— 10

MVP: **Jim Plunkett, QB, Oakland**

HEAD COACHES
OAKLAND: **Tom Flores**
PHILADELPHIA: **Dick Vermeil**

Super Bowl XVI

Joe Montana passed for one touchdown and ran for another in a game that pitted two Cinderella teams against each other. Each club had won only six games in 1980 before becoming its conference's surprise representative in the Super Bowl in '81. Each club also was playing in the Super Bowl for the first time.

Montana, San Francisco's third-year quarterback, made sure it was the 49ers who won their first title. He completed five of six passes on San Francisco's first drive, and capped the 11-play, 68-yard march with a one-yard quarterback sneak for a touchdown. In the second quarter, he finished off a 12-play, 92-yard drive by tossing an 11-yard scoring pass to fullback Earl Cooper for a 14-0 lead.

By halftime, the score was 20-0. The Bengals rallied in the second half, but the 49ers held on with the help of a dramatic goal-line stand in the third quarter. Cincinnati drove to a first-and-goal at the three-yard line, then failed to get into the end zone on three tries from inside the one.

Kicker Ray Wersching

■ *Montana's legend began here.*

**SAN FRANCISCO 49ERS 26,
CINCINNATI BENGALS 21**

January 24, 1982
Pontiac Silverdome • Pontiac, Michigan
ATTENDANCE: 81,270

San Francisco (NFC)	7	13	0	6 —	26
Cincinnati (AFC)	0	0	7	14 —	21

MVP: **Joe Montana, QB, San Francisco**

HEAD COACHES
SAN FRANCISCO: **Bill Walsh**
CINCINNATI: **Forrest Gregg**

played a key role for San Francisco. He not only equaled a Super Bowl record by kicking four field goals, but he also executed several squib kickoffs that bounced erratically on the artificial playing surface, forcing fumbles or pinning the Bengals deep.

Super Bowl XVI was the first to be played in the northern half of the United States. Each of the first 15 games had been played at warm-weather locales. Of course, XVI was played inside the climate-controlled atmosphere of the Pontiac Silverdome, which had been the home of the Detroit Lions since 1975.

The victory was the first of four Super Bowl titles for the 49ers in the 1980s.

■ *Riggins rambled the 'Skins to a win.*

Super Bowl XVII

Throughout the postseason, the Redskins put the ball in the hands of John Riggins and rode their rugged fullback to victory. So, with Super Bowl XVII on the line in the fourth quarter, it was no surprise that they did it again. Riggins responded by rushing 43 yards for the go-ahead touchdown in the final period of Washington's win over the Dolphins.

Miami generated little offense throughout the game, managing only 176 total yards, but the Dolphins took a 17-13 lead into the final period on the strength of several big plays. They included David Woodley's 76-yard touchdown pass to Jimmy Cefalo to open the scoring in the first quarter, Fulton Walker's 42-yard kickoff return to set up a field goal

in the second quarter, and Walker's 98-yard kickoff return for a touchdown 1:51 before halftime. It was the first kickoff return for a touchdown in Super Bowl history.

Early in the fourth quarter, Washington took over possession at its own 48-yard line. On fourth-and-1 from Miami's 43, the Redskins gave the ball to Riggins. He eluded cornerback Don McNeal's grasp at the line of the scrimmage, and burst into the clear around left end. Riggins raced all the way to the end zone to give the Redskins their first lead of the game. Washington put the game out of reach on its next possession when Joe Theismann tossed a six-yard touchdown pass to Charlie Brown with 1:55 left.

Riggins was named the game's MVP after rushing for 166 yards on 38 carries. It was his fourth consecutive 100-yard rushing day in the 1982 postseason.

WASHINGTON REDSKINS 27, MIAMI DOLPHINS 17

January 30, 1983

Rose Bowl • Pasadena, California

ATTENDANCE: 103,667

Miami (AFC)	7	10	0	0 —	17
Washington (NFC)	0	10	3	14 —	27

MVP: **John Riggins, RB, Washington**

HEAD COACHES
WASHINGTON: **Joe Gibbs**
MIAMI: **Don Shula**

Super Bowl XVIII

The defending-champion Redskins set an NFL record (since broken) for points scored during the regular season, but it was the Los Angeles Raiders who erupted on offense to win the Super Bowl for the third time in franchise history. Los Angeles' defense, meanwhile, limited Washington to a season-low nine points.

The critical play of the game came in the closing seconds of the first half, with the Raiders holding a 14-3 lead. The Redskins took over at their own 12-yard line with only 12 seconds left before intermission. Instead of running out the clock, though, Washington decided to try a pass play. Quarterback Joe Theismann flipped a short screen pass to his left in the direction of running back Joe Washington. But Theismann didn't see Raiders linebacker Jack Squirek in the same area until it was too late. Squirek stepped in front of the pass, intercepted it at the five-yard line, and walked into the end zone for a touchdown that broke the game wide open.

The Redskins tried to bounce back, scoring a touchdown on the opening possession of the second half when John Riggins capped a 70-yard drive with a one-yard run. But Los Angeles' Marcus Allen rushed for two touchdowns before the third quarter was finished to put the game out of reach.

■ *Allen's leaping runs added up to an MVP.*

The second was a 74-yard run on the last play of the period.

Washington had the NFL's top-ranked rushing defense during the regular season, but the awesome Allen amassed 191 yards on 20 carries in the Super Bowl. He was named the game's MVP.

LOS ANGELES RAIDERS 38, WASHINGTON REDSKINS 9

January 22, 1984

Tampa Stadium • Tampa, Florida

ATTENDANCE: 72,920

Washington (NFC)	0	3	6	0 — 9
L.A. Raiders (AFC)	7	14	14	3 — 38

MVP: **Marcus Allen, RB, L.A. Raiders**

HEAD COACHES
L.A. RAIDERS: **Tom Flores**
WASHINGTON: **Joe Gibbs**

Super Bowl XIX

The 49ers' offense rolled up 537 total yards, and their defense shut down Miami's high-powered attack in the second half. That added up to San Francisco's second Super Bowl championship in four years.

Quarterback Joe Montana paced the 49ers by completing 24 of 35 passes for 331 yards and three touchdowns. He ran for 59 yards and a score, too, to earn his second Super Bowl MVP award. Running back Roger Craig caught two of Montana's touchdown passes, and also ran for a touchdown.

Montana's performance outshined that of Miami's Dan Marino. The Dolphins' young quarterback, who set NFL records by passing

SAN FRANCISCO 49ERS 38, MIAMI DOLPHINS 16					
January 20, 1985					
Stanford Stadium • Stanford, California					
ATTENDANCE: 84,059					
Miami (AFC)	10	6	0	0	— 16
San Francisco (NFC)	7	21	10	0	— 38
MVP: Joe Montana, QB, San Francisco					
HEAD COACHES					
SAN FRANCISCO: **Bill Walsh**					
MIAMI: **Don Shula**					

for 5,084 yards and 48 touchdowns during the regular season, completed 29 of 50 passes for 318 yards. But he also was intercepted twice, sacked four times, fumbled once, and pressured throughout the game.

Marino did toss a two-yard touchdown pass to Dan Johnson in the final minute of the first quarter to put Miami ahead 10-7. But Montana's eight-yard touchdown pass to Craig 3:26 into the second period gave the 49ers the lead for good. They went on to score touchdowns on three consecutive possessions in the period to take a 28-16 lead at the half, and they were not threatened after that. Two second-half interceptions by the 49ers kept the Dolphins at a distance.

The victory capped an 18-1 season for the 49ers. Their only loss was a three-point defeat at home to Pittsburgh in the seventh game of the regular season.

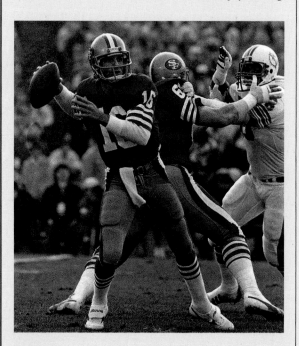

■ *Another MVP award for marvelous Montana.*

Super Bowl XX

The Bears' "46" Defense overwhelmed NFL opponents in 1985. So it was fitting that a fourth-quarter safety brought Chicago's total to 46 points in an overwhelming Super Bowl victory against the Patriots.

New England actually led this one early on, kicking a field goal for a 3-0 lead just 79 seconds into the contest. But even that field goal was indicative of things to come: The Patriots had to settle for three points because they failed to gain a yard after recovering a fumble at the Bears' 19-yard line. That was the way it went most of the afternoon for New England, which managed only 123 total yards, including a Super Bowl record-low seven yards on the ground. Starting quarterback Tony Eason did not complete a pass

■ *After scoring, the "Fridge" spiked the ball.*

in six attempts, was sacked three times, and lost a fumble. The Patriots netted minus-36 yards on Eason's six possessions before he gave way to backup Steve Grogan.

Chicago defensive end Richard Dent led the charge for Chicago. He had 1.5 sacks and forced a pair of fumbles to earn the MVP award. Linebacker Mike Singletary recovered two fumbles, and cornerback Reggie Phillips returned an interception for a touchdown.

On offense, quarterback Jim McMahon rushed for two touchdowns and passed for another. William "Refrigerator" Perry, a 335-pound defensive tackle, was inserted into the game at fullback and bulled his way into the end zone on a one-yard touchdown run.

CHICAGO BEARS 46, NEW ENGLAND PATRIOTS 10

January 26, 1986

Louisiana Superdome
New Orleans, Louisiana

ATTENDANCE: 73,818

Chicago (NFC)	13	10	21	2 —	46
New England (AFC)	3	0	0	7 —	10

MVP: **Richard Dent, DE, Chicago**

HEAD COACHES
CHICAGO: **Mike Ditka**
NEW ENGLAND: **Raymond Berry**

Super Bowl XXI

Quarterback Phil Simms was almost perfect while guiding the Giants to their first Super Bowl title. Simms completed 22 of his 25 passes for 268 yards and three touchdowns. His completion percentage of 88.0 is the best in Super Bowl history.

The Broncos, who were playing in the Super Bowl for the second time, held a 10-9 lead at the half behind quarterback John Elway. But New York took charge with a 17-point third quarter, then turned the game into a rout in the fourth period.

The momentum shifted on the opening drive of the second half. The Giants began the possession at their 37-yard line, but soon faced fourth-and-1 from the 46. The punting unit apparently jogged onto the field—but with backup quarterback Jeff Rutledge in

■ *Winning coach Parcells was carried off.*

place of a blocking back. Rutledge moved under center, took the snap, and snuck forward for two yards and a first down. Five plays later, Simms completed a six-yard touchdown pass to tight end Mark Bavaro to put New York in front.

Denver failed to make a first down any of the first three times it had the ball in the second half. The Giants, meanwhile, drove to a field goal and a touchdown after Broncos' punts, then converted cornerback Elvis Patterson's interception into a fourth-quarter touchdown that made the score 33-10.

By then, everything was going New York's way. The touchdown came when a pass bounced off Bavaro's hands and into the arms of wide receiver Phil McConkey.

NEW YORK GIANTS 39, DENVER BRONCOS 20

January 25, 1987

Rose Bowl • Pasadena, California

ATTENDANCE: 101,063

Denver (AFC)	10	0	0	10	— 20
N.Y. Giants (NFC)	7	2	17	13	— 39

MVP: **Phil Simms, QB, N.Y. Giants**

HEAD COACHES
N.Y. GIANTS: **Bill Parcells**
DENVER: **Dan Reeves**

Super Bowl XXII

In the most stunning turnaround in Super Bowl history, the Redskins erased an early 10-point deficit by erupting for 35 points in the second quarter to turn the game into a rout in their favor. Washington's remarkable outburst involved only 18 plays from scrimmage.

The stretch began when the Redskins took over at their 20-yard line in the opening minute of the second quarter. On the first play, quarterback Doug Williams teamed with wide receiver Ricky Sanders on an 80-yard touchdown pass. After the Broncos punted the ball back, Washington needed just five

WASHINGTON REDSKINS 42, DENVER BRONCOS 10

January 31, 1988

**San Diego Jack Murphy Stadium
San Diego, California**

ATTENDANCE: 73,302

Washington (NFC)	0	35	0	7 — 42
Denver (AFC)	10	0	0	0 — 10

MVP: **Doug Williams, QB, Washington**

HEAD COACHES
WASHINGTON: **Joe Gibbs**
DENVER: **Dan Reeves**

plays to march 64 yards, with the last 27 coming on Williams' touchdown pass to Gary Clark to put the Redskins ahead for good 10:15 before halftime.

Before the second quarter was over, Williams threw two more touchdown passes, and running back Timmy Smith burst 58 yards for another score. Smith, a rookie backup, didn't find out he was starting the Super Bowl in place of injured George Rogers until moments before the game. He gained 204 yards on 22 carries.

Williams, the game's MVP, completed 18 of 29 passes for 340 yards and four touchdowns. He was the first African-American quarterback to start a Super Bowl. His main target was Sanders, who was on the receiving end of nine of Williams's passes for 193 yards and two scores.

■ *Williams made Super Bowl history.*

■ *Rice's 215 yards is still a Super Bowl record.*

Super Bowl XXIII

The 49ers beat the Bengals in one of the most thrilling finishes in Super Bowl history. The winning score came when Joe Montana tossed a 10-yard TD pass to John Taylor with just 34 seconds left. It is the only time that the lead has changed hands in the final minute of a Super Bowl game.

San Francisco dominated the game statistically, nearly doubling Cincinnati in total yards gained (453 to 229). But when Jim Breech kicked his third field goal of the game, from 40 yards with 3:20 remaining in the fourth quarter, the Bengals led, 16-13.

A penalty on the ensuing kickoff meant that the 49ers had to begin their final possession on their own eight-yard line. Montana went to work, quickly completing three short passes to move the ball out to the 30. After a couple of short runs, a 17-yard pass to Jerry Rice moved the ball into Cincinnati territory.

The key play of the drive came after a penalty left San Francisco faced with a second-and-20 from the Bengals' 45-yard line. Jerry Rice caught Montana's pass in stride over the middle and reached the 18-yard line before he was tackled. After a short pass to Roger Craig, Montana teamed with Taylor for the winning score.

Montana completed 7 of 8 passes on the decisive drive and finished 23 of 36 for 357 yards for the game. The game's MVP award, though, went to Rice. He set a record that still stands when he amassed 215 yards on 11 catches, including a 14-yard touchdown early in the fourth quarter.

SAN FRANCISCO 49ERS 20, CINCINNATI BENGALS 16

January 22, 1989

Joe Robbie Stadium • Miami, Florida

ATTENDANCE: 75,129

Cincinnati (AFC)	0	3	10	3 — 16
San Francisco (NFC)	3	0	3	14 — 20

MVP: **Jerry Rice, WR, San Francisco**

HEAD COACHES:
SAN FRANCISCO: **Bill Walsh**
CINCINNATI: **Sam Wyche**

Super Bowl XXIV

The 49ers rolled to their second consecutive NFL title (and their fourth in nine seasons) behind the biggest scoring display in Super Bowl history. San Francisco's 45-point margin of victory also made this the most-lopsided Super Bowl ever.

The 49ers were in control from the start. After forcing Denver to punt on the game's opening possession, they needed only 10 plays to march 66 yards to a touchdown. Quarterback Joe Montana's 20-yard scoring pass to wide receiver Jerry Rice capped the drive and gave San Francisco a lead it would not give up. The 49ers went on to score two touchdowns in each quarter. They finished with overwhelming advantages in first downs (28 to 12) and total yards (461 to 167).

Montana set a Super Bowl record (since broken) by passing for five touchdowns, including three to Rice. In all, Montana completed 22 of 29 passes for 297 yards. He became the first (and still only) player to earn the Super Bowl MVP award three times. Rice had 7 receptions for 148 yards. Burly 49ers fullback Tom Rathman added two short scoring runs.

The 49ers became just the second team to win four Super Bowls. The AFC's Pittsburgh Steelers also won four titles in the six-season span from 1974 to 1979. Meanwhile,

■ *Rice and the 49ers bowled over Denver.*

Denver's futility in the big game continued. The Broncos lost the Super Bowl for the fourth time in as many tries, and for the third time in the last four seasons.

SAN FRANCISCO 49ERS 55, DENVER BRONCOS 10

January 28, 1990

**Louisiana Superdome
New Orleans, Louisiana**

ATTENDANCE: 72,919

San Francisco (NFC) 13 14 14 14 — 55
Denver (AFC)   3   0   7 0 — 10

MVP: **Joe Montana, QB, San Francisco**

HEAD COACHES:
SAN FRANCISCO: **George Seifert**
DENVER: **Dan Reeves**

Super Bowl XXV

In one of the most memorable Super Bowls ever, the New York Giants held on to win when Buffalo kicker Scott Norwood narrowly missed a long field-goal try in the closing seconds.

New York won by sticking to a game plan designed to keep the ball the ball away from the Bills' offense. Buffalo's no-huddle attack had confused defenses all season long, and often resulted in quick-strike touchdowns. But the Giants reasoned that the Bills couldn't score if they didn't have the ball. So they relied on the running of game MVP Ottis Anderson and the precision passing of quarterback Jeff Hostetler to maintain ball control. It worked: Anderson rushed for 102 yards on 21 carries, Hostetler completed 20 of 32 passes for 222 yards, and New York

■*Hostetler led a ball-hogging Giants offense.*

maintained possession of the ball for 40:33 of the game's 60 minutes.

The Giants executed their plan to perfection on the opening drive of the second half. Trailing 12-10, New York held the ball for 14 plays on a 75-yard drive that took nine minutes and 29 seconds. Along the way, the Giants converted four third-down opportunities into first downs. The biggest was Hostetler's short pass to Mark Ingram on third-and-13 from the Bills' 32-yard line. Ingram broke a couple of tackles and weaved his way for 14 yards and a first down. Five plays later, Anderson capped the march with a one-yard touchdown run to put the Giants ahead.

The Bills went back ahead when Thur-

NEW YORK GIANTS 20, BUFFALO BILLS 19

January 27, 1991

Tampa Stadium • Tampa, Florida

ATTENDANCE: 73,813

Buffalo (AFC)	3	9	0	7 —	19
N.Y. Giants (NFC)	3	7	7	3 —	20

MVP: **Ottis Anderson, RB, N.Y. Giants**

HEAD COACHES
N.Y. GIANTS: **Bill Parcells**
BUFFALO: **Marv Levy**

man Thomas, who gained 135 yards on just 15 carries, ran 31 yards for a touchdown on the first play of the fourth quarter. But New York countered with another lengthy march. Beginning from their 23-yard line, the Giants held the ball for 14 plays on a drive that consumed 7:32 of the fourth quarter. Matt Bahr's field goal capped the 74-yard march and gave New York a one-point lead with 7:20 remaining.

After an exchange of punts, Buffalo got the ball for one last time at its 10-yard line with 2:16 left. Thomas ran for 22 yards on a draw to pick up one first down, and quarterback Jim Kelly scrambled for nine yards to pick up another. Then, from the Giants' 40-yard line, Thomas burst 11 yards for another first down at the 29. After a spike to stop the clock with eight seconds left, Norwood came on to try a 47-yard field goal. But the kick sailed just wide to the right.

■ *Nearly a hero: Scott Norwood walks off after his fateful miss.*

Super Bowl XXVI

The Redskins won the Super Bowl for the third time in the last 10 years while handing the Bills their second consecutive defeat in the big game. Washington's three wins all came under head coach Joe Gibbs, but all came with a different starting quarterback at the helm.

Mark Rypien was the Redskins' quarterback in this one, and he came through with an MVP performance. Rypien completed 18 of 33 passes for 292 yards and two touchdowns against the Bills. He followed in the footsteps of a pair of previous Washington Super Bowl-winning signal callers Joe Theismann (XVII) and Doug Williams (XXII).

Rypien's first scoring pass was a 10-yard strike to running back Earnest Byner for the game's first touchdown 5:06 into the second quarter. Two plays later, veteran cornerback Darrell Green intercepted Jim Kelly's pass at the Redskins' 45-yard line. Rypien's 34-yard completion and Ricky Ervins' 14-yard run set up a one-yard touchdown run by Gerald Riggs that made the score 17-0 with 7:17 still to play in the second quarter.

It stayed that way until halftime, and then the

■ *MVP Rypien celebrates after one of his two TD passes.*

■ *Veteran Art Monk had 113 receiving yards.*

Clark (114 yards on seven catches) and Art Monk (113 yards on seven catches) each posted 100-yard pass-catching days for the Redskins. Ervins added a game-high 72 yards rushing as Washington amassed 417 total yards.

Buffalo's Kelly attempted a Super Bowl-record 58 passes while trying to rally his team. He completed 28 of his throws for 275 yards and a pair of touchdowns, but he also was intercepted four times, was sacked five times, and lost a fumble. The Bills' high-powered offense was limited to 283 total yards.

The Redskins' Gibbs joined Pittsburgh's Chuck Noll (four wins) and San Francisco's Bill Walsh (three) as the third coach to win the Super Bowl three times. Gibbs was the first to accomplish the feat using three different starting quarterbacks.

Redskins put the game out of reach in the opening seconds of the third quarter. On the first play of the second half, linebacker Kurt Gouveia intercepted Kelly's pass and returned the ball 23 yards to the Bills' two-yard line. Riggs bulled his way for another touchdown on the next play to make it 24-0 after only 16 seconds of the period.

Buffalo briefly closed to within 14 points, but Rypien answered with a 30-yard touchdown pass to Clark. The Redskins went on to lead by as many as 27 points before the Bills scored two touchdowns late in the game.

WASHINGTON REDSKINS 37, BUFFALO BILLS 24

January 26, 1992

**Hubert H. Humphrey Metrodome
Minneapolis, Minnesota**

ATTENDANCE: 63,130

Washington (NFC)	0 17 14 6 — 37		
Buffalo (AFC)	0 0 10 14 — 24		

MVP: **Mark Rypien, QB, Washington**

**HEAD COACHES
WASHINGTON: Joe Gibbs
BUFFALO: Marv Levy**

Super Bowl XXVII

Only three years removed from a one-win season, the Cowboys completed their turnaround by reaching the top of the NFL world. They had no trouble handing the Bills their third consecutive loss in the Super Bowl.

MVP Troy Aikman led Dallas' balanced attack by passing for 273 yards and four touchdowns, while running back Emmitt Smith gained 108 yards and scored a touchdown on the ground. Michael Irvin amassed 114 yards receiving and had a pair of scoring catches for the Cowboys, who outgained the Bills 408 yards to 362.

Turnovers were the real difference in the game, though. Buffalo committed a whopping nine of them, the most ever in a Super Bowl. The Bills lost five fumbles and had four passes intercepted. The first of them came late in the first quarter, with Buffalo holding its only lead of the game at 7-0.

With the ball at midfield, Bills quarterback Jim Kelly was hit by the Dallas pass rushers as threw a pass intended for tight end Pete Metzelaars. Dallas safety James Washington picked off the errant throw and returned the ball to Buffalo's 47-yard line. Six plays later, Aikman teamed with tight end Jay Novacek on a 23-yard touchdown pass to tie the game.

On the very next play from scrimmage, Kelly dropped back to pass from his 10-yard line, but was sacked by Cowboys defensive end Charles Haley. The ball popped loose, and the fumble was grabbed by big Dallas defensive tackle Jimmie Jones, who ran two yards for a touchdown that put Dallas ahead for good.

Those two touchdowns came just 15 seconds apart late in the first quarter. The Cowboys struck twice again almost as quickly—in 18 seconds—to break the game open late in the second period. First, Smith's 38-yard run preceded Aikman's 19-yard scoring strike to Irvin 1:54 before halftime. Then, again on the next play from scrimmage, Buffalo running back Thurman Thomas lost a fumble at the Bills' 18-yard line. Aikman immediately tossed another touchdown pass to Irvin to put Dallas ahead 28-10.

DALLAS COWBOYS 52, BUFFALO BILLS 17

January 31, 1993

Rose Bowl • Pasadena, California

ATTENDANCE: 98,374

Buffalo (AFC)	7	3	7	0 — 17
Dallas (NFC)	14	14	3	21 — 52

MVP: **Troy Aikman, QB, Dallas**

HEAD COACHES
DALLAS: **Jimmy Johnson**
BUFFALO: **Marv Levy**

In the fourth quarter, the Cowboys scored 21 points in a span of less than three minutes to pull away. Another interception and another fumble recovery led to 14 of the points. In all, Dallas scored 35 points following Buffalo turnovers.

The Cowboys won the Super Bowl for the third time in six appearances in the big game. It was Dallas' first NFL title since beating Denver in Super Bowl XII.

The Cowboys' return to the top came after a stormy period following Jerry Jones' purchase of the club from former owner Bum Bright in January of 1989. Jones immediately hired Jimmy Johnson, his former college teammate, to replace Tom Landry as head coach. Johnson had been a very successful college coach, but the enormously popular Landry was the only coach Dallas ever had to that point. Four years later, Johnson had Dallas back on top.

■ *Score one for the defense: Jones leaps to score over Kelly.*

Super Bowl XXVIII

The Bills became the only team ever to play in the Super Bowl four years in a row, but they also lost for the fourth consecutive year. In a rematch of the previous Super Bowl, the Cowboys won their second in a row and their fourth overall. This one was close until MVP Emmitt Smith took over the game in the second half for Dallas.

Buffalo, in fact, led 13-6 at halftime on the strength of two field goals by Steve Christie (one a Super Bowl-record 54-yarder) and Thurman Thomas' four-yard touchdown run. The Bills got the ball first in the second half, too, and were driving near midfield. But Thomas lost a fumble when he was hit by Dallas' Leon Lett. Safety James Washington picked up the ball and raced 46 yards down the left sideline for the game-tying TD.

■ *The powerful, elusive MVP Smith helped Dallas control the ball for long periods.*

The next time the Cowboys had possession, Smith ran the ball seven times on an eight-play drive to the go-ahead score. He gained 61 of the 64 yards on the march, including the last 15 yards for a touchdown that gave Dallas a 20-13 lead.

Buffalo never seriously threatened after that. The Bills punted each of the next two times they had the ball before Washington intercepted quarterback Jim Kelly's pass on the first play of the fourth quarter. It took the Cowboys nine plays to cover 34 yards and turn Washington's theft into a touchdown. Smith carried the ball six times and caught a pass on the short march. His one-yard touchdown run with 9:50 remaining in the game made it 27-13.

Smith ran the ball on 20 of the Cowboys' 34 plays from scrimmage in the second half. In all, he finished with 30 carries for 132 yards. Quarterback Troy Aikman added 207 yards through the air on 19 completions in 27 attempts. On defense, Washington had a spectacular day with 11 tackles, an interception, a fumble recovery, and a forced fumble. Kelly completed 31 of 50 passes for 260 yards for Buffalo. Washington was primarily a reserve for the Cowboys in 1993, but he played most of the game as the Cowboys attempted to stop the Bills' No-Huddle offense.

Dallas became the first team in NFL history to win the Super Bowl after losing its

DALLAS COWBOYS 30, BUFFALO BILLS 13

January 30, 1994
Georgia Dome • Atlanta, Georgia
ATTENDANCE: 72,817

Dallas (NFC)	6	0	14	10	— 30
Buffalo (AFC)	3	10	0	0	— 13

MVP: **Emmitt Smith, RB, Dallas**

HEAD COACHES
DALLAS: **Jimmy Johnson**
BUFFALO: **Marv Levy**

first two games of the regular season. An NFC team won the Super Bowl for the 10th season in row.

The Cowboys had stumbled out of the gate in 1993 by getting blown out 35-16 by division-rival Washington, then losing to Buffalo 13-10 in their home opener. Not coincidentally, Smith missed those two games while in a contract dispute with team ownership. The all-time rushing leader had set club records (which he eventually broke) the year before by rushing for 1,713 yards and scoring 19 touchdowns.

With the money issues resolved, Smith returned to the lineup, and Dallas began a seven-game winning streak. The Cowboys went on to finish the season 12-4. Despite playing in only 14 games, Smith led the NFL by rushing for 1,486 yards while scoring 10 touchdowns.

Super Bowl XXIX

Quarterback Steve Young and the 49ers' offense were unstoppable in a rout of the Chargers. With the victory, San Francisco became the first franchise to win the Super Bowl five times.

Young, a backup to Joe Montana on the 49ers' NFL championship teams in the 1988 and 1989 seasons, broke his former teammate's Super Bowl record by passing for six touchdowns against San Diego. Young completed 24 of 36 passes for 325 yards, led all runners with 49 yards on the ground, and was named the game's MVP. Jerry Rice, who caught 10 passes for 149 yards, was Young's primary target. Rice equaled his own Super Bowl record by catching three scoring passes. Running back Ricky Watters had two touchdown receptions.

SAN FRANCISCO 49ERS 49, SAN DIEGO CHARGERS 26

January 29, 1995
Joe Robbie Stadium • Miami, Florida
ATTENDANCE: 74,107

San Diego (AFC)	7	3	8	8 —	26
San Francisco (NFC)	14	14	14	7 —	49

MVP: **Steve Young, QB, San Francisco**

HEAD COACHES
SAN FRANCISCO: **George Seifert**
SAN DIEGO: **Bobby Ross**

San Francisco wasted no time getting on the scoreboard. On the third play of the game, Young dropped back to pass and found Rice streaking down the middle of the field, behind the Chargers' defense. Rice caught Young's throw and raced into the end zone. The next time the 49ers had the ball, they needed only four plays to score. After Young scrambled 21 yards for a first down to the 49-yard line, he completed a 51-yard scoring strike to Watters. That gave San Francisco a 14-0 lead only 4:55 into the game.

San Diego tried to keep it close by responding with its most impressive drive of the game. Behind the running of Natrone Means and the passing of quarterback Stan Humphries, the Chargers marched 78 yards in 13 plays. They pulled within seven points on Means' one-yard touchdown run with 2:44 still to play in the opening quarter.

The touchdown could not stop the deluge, however. The 49ers countered with a 70-yard drive capped by Young's five-yard touchdown pass to fullback William Floyd, and the rout was on. San Francisco went on to score touchdowns on four of its first five possessions and had a 28-10 advantage at halftime.

Humphries passed for 275 yards and a touchdown for San Diego. But Means, who gained 1,350 yards during the regular season, ran only 13 times for 33 yards—with 26

■ Young moved out of the shadows and into the spotlight for good.

of the yards coming in the first quarter. The Chargers were outgained 449 total yards to 354.

The 75 total points scored by the two teams remains the most in Super Bowl history.

The victory was especially sweet for Young. He had been acquired by San Francisco via trade from Tampa Bay in 1987, and spent several seasons in a reserve role behind Montana. In 1991, he took over as the starter after Montana was injured. By 1993, Montana was healthy, but the job was Young's. So the 49ers traded Montana to Kansas City—and many San Francisco followers were lukewarm in their support of Young as a result.

En route to the NFC title in 1994, he passed for 3,969 yards and 35 touchdowns while breaking Montana's single-season record with a passer rating of 112.8. (Peyton Manning has since broken Young's mark.)

Super Bowl XXX

The Cowboys won the Super Bowl for the third time in four years by jumping out to an early lead, then holding off the Steelers with a couple of big plays on defense in the second half. Those plays were interceptions from cornerback Larry Brown, who set up 14 points with his thefts and earned the game's MVP award.

Dallas never trailed after taking the opening kickoff and marching 47 yards to Chris Boniol's 42-yard field goal. After Pittsburgh didn't make a first down on its initial possession and punted, the Cowboys drove 75 yards to a touchdown. Quarterback Troy Aikman's three-yard pass to tight end Jay Novacek upped the advantage to 10-0. Boniol added another field on Dallas' third possession to make it 13-0.

It was 13-7 midway through the third quarter when Brown made his first interception. He picked off Neil O'Donnell's pass at the Cowboys' 38-yard line and returned it all the way to Pittsburgh's 18. After Aikman completed a 17-yard pass to Michael Irvin, Emmitt Smith ran one yard for a touchdown.

The Steelers never gave up, though, and trailed just 20-17 when they took over the ball at their 32-yard line with 4:15 remaining. On second down, Brown intercepted O'Donnell again. Two plays later, Smith's

DALLAS COWBOYS 27, PITTSBURGH STEELERS 17

January 28, 1996

Sun Devil Stadium • Tempe, Arizona

ATTENDANCE: 76,347

Dallas (NFC)	10	3	7	7 – 27
Pittsburgh (AFC)	0	7	0	10 – 17

MVP: Larry Brown, CB, Dallas

HEAD COACHES
DALLAS: Barry Switzer
PITTSBURGH: Bill Cowher

four-yard touchdown run sealed the deal.

Smith, who led the NFL with 1,773 rushing yards during the regular season, was held in check by Pittsburgh's defense. After a 23-yard run on his first carry, he gained just 26 yards on 17 attempts the rest of the way, although he did have the two scoring runs. Aikman completed 15 of 23 passes for 209 yards. O'Donnell passed for 239 yards and a touchdown for the Steelers, who outgained Dallas 310 total yards to 254.

The Cowboys won the Super Bowl for the fifth time in franchise history. They equaled the 49ers for the most all-time Super Bowl wins. It was Dallas' first Super Bowl win under second-year coach Barry Switzer. He joined Jimmy Johnson, the man who preceded him with the Cowboys, as the only coaches to win a Super Bowl and a college national championship.

■ *Pittsburgh's Bam Morris was roped in by a host of Cowboys; the Dallas D excelled in this game.*

Super Bowl XXXI

After 29 years, the Packers made a triumphant return to the Super Bowl by beating the Patriots. Green Bay had not played in the Super Bowl since winning games I and II in the 1966 and 1967 seasons. And they made "return" the theme of the game as special teams plays turned out to be the key moments of the game.

Quarterback Brett Favre keyed the Green Bay offense by passing for 246 yards and two touchdowns and also running for another score. But it was kick-return specialist Desmond Howard who provided the key spark and was named the game's most valuable player.

Howard, the 1991 Heisman Trophy winner while in college at Michigan, had found little success as an NFL wide receiver with the Redskins and Jaguars. But he signed with the Packers as a free agent in 1996 and led the league with an average of 15.1 yards per punt return during the regular season that year.

On his first chance in the Super Bowl, Howard returned a punt 32 yards to Green Bay's 45-yard line. Two plays later, Favre teamed with wide receiver Andre Rison on a 54-yard touchdown

■ What's Howard watching? Himself on a stadium video screen.

■ *Favre shared his joy with the Packers' faithful fans.*

Favre completed 14 of 27 passes, including an 81-yard touchdown strike to wide receiver Antonio Freeman that put the Packers ahead for good at 17-14 in the second quarter. At the time, it was the longest play from scrimmage in Super Bowl history.

Drew Bledsoe completed 25 of 48 passes for 253 yards and two touchdowns for the Patriots. But he also was intercepted four times and sacked five times. Green Bay defensive end Reggie White set a Super Bowl record that still stands by posting three of the sacks.

The Packers' victory was the 13th in a row by an NFC team over an AFC team in the Super Bowl.

pass to put the Packers ahead just 3:32 into the game. Howard would go on to return six punts for 90 yards and four kickoffs for 154 yards in the game. The biggest was a 99-yard kickoff return for a touchdown late in the third quarter. It came after New England had pulled within 27-21 on Curtis Martin's 18-yard touchdown run, and it broke the Patriots' spirit. New England made just one first down the rest of the way and never advanced the ball past its own 39-yard line.

After the game, Howard revealed that he had had a little help eluding Patriots defenders on the play. As he raced away from the trailing Pats, Howard watched himself live on a giant video screen above the end zone directly in front of him.

GREEN BAY PACKERS 35, NEW ENGLAND PATRIOTS 21

January 26, 1997

Louisiana Superdome
New Orleans, Louisiana

ATTENDANCE: 72,301

New England (AFC)	14	0	7	0	— 21
Green Bay (NFC)	10	17	8	0	— 35

MVP: **Desmond Howard, KR-PR, Green Bay**

HEAD COACHES
GREEN BAY: **Mike Holmgren**
NEW ENGLAND: **Bill Parcells**

Super Bowl XXXII

In their fifth appearance in the Super Bowl, the Broncos broke through for their first victory with an upset of the Packers. Denver's win ended Green Bay's quest for a second consecutive Super Bowl title, and it snapped the NFC's 13-game winning streak in the big game.

Running back Terrell Davis was the star for the Broncos. He gained 157 yards on the ground and scored three touchdowns, including the decisive one-yard run with 1:45 left in the game. After that, Denver still had to hold off one final push by the Packers. Beginning from its 30-yard line, Green

DENVER BRONCOS 31, GREEN BAY PACKERS 24

January 25, 1998

**Qualcomm Stadium
San Diego, California**

ATTENDANCE: 68,912

Green Bay (NFC)	7	7	3	7	24
Denver (AFC)	7	10	7	7	31

MVP: **Terrell Davis, RB, Denver**

**HEAD COACHES
DENVER: Mike Shanahan
GREEN BAY: Mike Holmgren**

Bay quickly drove to Denver's 35-yard line on completions of 22 yards and 13 yards from quarterback Brett Favre to running back Dorsey Levens. But on fourth down from the 31, Favre's pass intended for tight end Mark Chmura was batted away by linebacker John Mobley. That sealed the outcome and set off a celebration on the Broncos' sideline.

Davis, who carried the ball 30 times, also had one-yard scoring runs in the first and third quarters. The latter came in the final minute of the period and capped a 13-play, 92-yard march that put Denver ahead 24-17 in the

■ *MVP for TD: Davis made like his initials with three scores.*

back-and-forth game. After an exchange of turnovers, the Packers countered by driving to the tying touchdown, which came on Favre's 13-yard touchdown pass to Antonio Freeman 1:28 into the final period.

The score remained tied at 24-24 until Denver took possession with 3:27 to go at the Packers' 49-yard line following a punt. From the 18, Davis burst 17 yards to set up his winning run.

Broncos quarterback John Elway, starting for the fourth time in a Super Bowl, was not called on to pass much. He completed 12 of 22 attempts for a modest 123 yards. But his completions included a 36-yard strike to Ed McCaffrey to set up

■ *Finally! Veteran John Elway ended his Super Bowl jinx.*

Davis' second touchdown run late in the third quarter, as well as a 23-yard pass to fullback Howard Griffith on the game-winning drive in the fourth quarter.

Elway also ran one yard for a touchdown on the opening play of the second quarter to give Denver its first lead of the game at 14-7.

Favre completed 25 of 42 passes for 256 yards and three touchdowns for Green Bay. Freeman amassed 126 yards on nine catches, including two for scores.

The victory gave the Broncos their first championship in the 38-year history of the franchise. Denver was one of the original members of the AFL in 1960.

Super Bowl XXXIII

Quarterback John Elway capped his long and glorious NFL career in style, leading the Broncos to the victory. It was Denver's second consecutive Super Bowl title, and thwarted the Falcons' quest for their first championship.

A year earlier, Elway had contemplated retiring after the Broncos beat the Packers in Super Bowl XXXII in the 1997 season. That game had ended his career-long Super Bowl drought. But he decided to come back for one more year, and he became the only man ever to earn Super Bowl MVP honors in his final game. The 16-year veteran played a more active role against the Falcons than he did the previous year against Green Bay, when he mostly handed off to running back Terrell Davis. Davis, who became just the

DENVER BRONCOS 34, ATLANTA FALCONS 19

January 31, 1999

Pro Player Stadium • Miami, Florida

ATTENDANCE: 74,803

Denver (AFC)	7	10	0	17 —	34
Atlanta (NFC)	3	3	0	13 —	19

MVP: **John Elway, QB, Denver**

HEAD COACHES
DENVER: **Mike Shanahan**
ATLANTA: **Dan Reeves**

fourth man in NFL history to run for more than 2,000 yards during the regular season (he had 2,008), did gain 102 yards on 25 carries in this one. But Elway was the star of the show this time around. The 38-year-old completed 18 of 29 passes for 336 yards, and he ran for another touchdown.

The game's key segment came in the second quarter, with Denver leading 10-3. Atlanta marched to the Broncos' eight-yard line, but the Falcons came away empty when the usually reliable kicker Morten Andersen missed a 26-yard field-goal try. On the next play, Elway found wide receiver Rod Smith streaking behind Atlanta's secondary. The two teamed on a back-breaking 80-yard touchdown strike that upped Denver's advantage to 17-3.

The game turned into a rout in the second half. Denver cornerback Darrien Gordon intercepted Falcons quarterback Chris Chandler on back-to-back possessions inside Denver territory, returning the thefts 58 and 50 yards. The first led to fullback Howard Griffith's second touchdown run, and the second set up Elway's three-yard touchdown run that made it 31-6 with 11:20 left to play.

Tim Dwight provided the big highlight for Atlanta when he returned the ensuing kickoff 94 yards for a touchdown, but the outcome was pretty much decided by then.

■ *Am I in? Yep, you're in the end zone, John, and on your way to the Hall of Fame.*

Chandler led the Falcons by passing for 219 yards and a touchdown, but he also was sacked twice and intercepted three times. Young running star Jamal Anderson gained 96 yards on 18 carries. Atlanta was coached by Dan Reeves, the man who led the Broncos to three Super Bowl appearances in a four-year span of the 1980s.

Following the game, Elway basked in the much-deserved attention. He had not needed one of his patented come-from-behind drives to carry Denver to this victory, but he would relish it like no other. He didn't officially announce his retirement until later that spring, but everyone at the game knew that they had seen the fitting end of the Elway legend.

Super Bowl XXXIV

The Rams held off the Titans to win the Super Bowl for the first time. It was the Rams' first NFL championship since the 1951 season, when the club was based in Los Angeles.

This game featured one of the most exciting finishes in Super Bowl history. Trailing by seven points in the final seconds, the Titans drove to St. Louis' 10-yard line with time for one more play. Tennessee quarterback Steve McNair completed a short pass to wide receiver Kevin Dyson over the middle. Dyson reached for the end zone, but was tackled by linebacker Mike Jones a yard short of the goal line as time ran out. The dramatic end-

ST. LOUIS RAMS 23, TENNESSEE TITANS 16				
January 30, 2000				
Georgia Dome • Atlanta, Georgia				
ATTENDANCE: 72,625				
St. Louis (NFC)	3	6	7	7 – 23
Tennessee (AFC)	0	0	6	10 – 16
MVP: **Kurt Warner, QB, St. Louis**				
HEAD COACHES				
ST. LOUIS: **Dick Vermeil**				
TENNESSEE: **Jeff Fisher**				

ing spoiled a big comeback for the Titans, who had rallied from a 16-0 deficit in the second half.

During the 1999 regular season, St. Louis featured one of the most explosive of-

■ *So close and yet so far: Dyson stretched for the tying score, but Jones made the saving tackle.*

fenses in NFL history. The Rams' 526 points that year was the third-most in a season ever. They had little trouble moving the ball against Tennessee in the Super Bowl. In fact, St. Louis marched inside the Titans' 20-yard line on each of its first six possessions. But the Rams had to settle for three short field goals by Jeff Wilkins before scoring their first touchdown on a nine-yard pass from quarterback Kurt Warner to wide receiver Torry Holt. That gave St. Louis its 16-point advantage with 7:20 left in the third quarter.

Then the Titans' offense came to life. Beginning at its 34-yard line, Tennessee marched 66 yards in 12 plays, the last being Eddie George's one-yard touchdown run 14 seconds before the end of the third quarter. A two-point conversion attempt failed, but the Titans soon embarked on another long drive early in the fourth period. That march covered 79 yards in 13 plays, with George's two-yard run pulling them within 16-13. After a short punt, Tennessee pulled even on Al Del Greco's 43-yard field goal with 2:12 left in the game.

In a little more than 20 minutes of playing time, the Rams had been outscored 16-0 while gaining only one yard from scrimmage (to Tennessee's 173) and maintaining possession for only 1:42 (to Tennessee's 18:26). But St. Louis needed only one play to swing the game in its favor. On first down from the

■ *A happy champ with the Super Bowl trophy.*

Rams' 27-yard line, Warner tossed a long pass to Isaac Bruce at the Titans' 38. Bruce raced to the end zone to complete a 73-yard touchdown pass that proved to be the winning points.

Warner, who had already won the 1999 NFL MVP award despite the fact that he had never started a game prior to the season, was named the game's MVP after passing for a Super Bowl-record 414 yards. Bruce (162 yards on six catches) and Holt (109 yards on seven catches) each had 100-yard receiving days. McNair passed for 214 yards, and George rushed for 95 yards for Tennessee.

Super Bowl XXXV

The Ravens' record-setting defense suffocated opponents during the regular season and the AFC playoffs. So it was little surprise when that unit carried the club past the Giants to win the Super Bowl for the first time in franchise history.

Baltimore allowed a meager 165 total points during the 2000 regular season. It was the lowest mark by an NFL team since the league went to a 16-game schedule in 1978. Then, in the postseason, the Ravens were even better, permitting a combined 16 points in victories over Denver, Tennessee, and Oakland to reach the Super Bowl. Against the Giants, Baltimore did not allow an offensive touchdown and limited New York to only 152 total yards while posting four sacks and recording five takeaways.

The Giants managed only 11 first downs and did not drive inside Baltimore's 29-yard line. Their lone points came when Ron Dixon returned a kickoff 97 yards for a touchdown with 3:31 left in the third quarter.

Dixon's big return pulled New York within 17-7—but only briefly. That's because Baltimore's Jermaine Lewis countered with an 84-yard return on the ensuing kickoff to re-establish a 17-point lead for the Ravens. Lewis' return capped a 21-point scoring spree in a span of 36 seconds, with all of the points coming on defense or special teams. Baltimore cornerback Duane Starks began the

■ *Coach Brian Billick takes a chilly victory bath.*

■ *Baltimore's Lewis earned the first MVP award for a defender since Super Bowl XX.*

spurt by intercepting Kerry Collins' pass and returning it 49 yards for a touchdown.

Lewis, who amassed 145 yards on all returns, also brought back a punt 34 yards in

BALTIMORE RAVENS 34, NEW YORK GIANTS 7

January 28, 2001

Raymond James Stadium
Tampa, Florida

ATTENDANCE: **71,921**

Baltimore (AFC)	7	3	14	10 —	34
N.Y. Giants (NFC)	0	0	7	0 —	7

MVP: **Ray Lewis, LB, Baltimore**

HEAD COACHES
BALTIMORE: **Brian Billick**
N.Y. GIANTS: **Jim Fassel**

the first quarter. That set up the game's first score, which came on Trent Dilfer's 38-yard touchdown pass to Brandon Stokley 8:10 into the game.

Dilfer passed for 153 yards, and Jamal Lewis (no relation to Jermaine) rushed for 102 yards for the Ravens, who asked little of their offense. Linebacker Ray Lewis (no relation to Jermaine or Jamal) was named the game's most valuable player. He had just five tackles and four passes defensed, but proved to be the heart and soul of Baltimore's defense all season. Lewis and the rest of Baltimore's defense harassed Collins throughout the game. The Giants' quarterback completed only 15 of his 39 pass attempts for 112 yards. He was intercepted four times.

■ *V for Vinatieri . . . and for victory!*

Super Bowl XXXVI

The Patriots shocked the heavily favored Rams to win the Super Bowl for the first time. New England kept St. Louis' high-flying offense out of the end zone until the fourth quarter, then won the game with a field goal as time ran out.

The Rams' offense was nicknamed "The

NEW ENGLAND PATRIOTS 20, ST. LOUIS RAMS 17					

February 3, 2002

**Louisiana Superdome
New Orleans, Louisiana**

ATTENDANCE: 72,922

St. Louis (NFC)	3	0	0	14	— 17
New England (AFC)	0	14	3	3	— 20

MVP: **Tom Brady, QB, New England**

HEAD COACHES
NEW ENGLAND: **Bill Belichick**
ST. LOUIS: **Mike Martz**

Greatest Show on Turf" for its ability to light up the scoreboard. But the Patriots, behind a defense designed by head coach Bill Belichick, frustrated St. Louis in the Super Bowl and built a 17-3 lead through three quarters by scoring two touchdowns and a field goal following Rams' turnovers. Cornerback Ty Law returned set the tone when he intercepted Warner's pass midway through the second quarter and returned the ball 47 yards for a touchdown to put New England ahead 7-3.

Late in the first half, defensive back Terrell Buckley recovered wide receiver Ricky Proehl's fumble in Patriots' territory. That led to young quarterback Tom Brady's eight-yard scoring pass to David Patten. Brady had taken over the starting job when veteran Drew Bledsoe, who had guided the Patriots to Super Bowl XXXI in the 1996 season, was injured early in the year. A sixth-round draft choice out of Michigan in 2000, Brady played so well that he kept the job even after Bledsoe came back healthy.

After cornerback Otis Smith intercepted Warner's pass, Adam Vinatieri kicked a 37-yard field goal late in the third quarter to increase New England's advantage to 14 points. Then the Rams got their offense going.

First, Warner capped a 77-yard drive by running two yards for a touchdown 5:29 into the fourth quarter. Then, after the Patriots failed to generate a first down on either of their next two possessions, Warner's 26-yard touchdown pass to Proehl tied the score with 1:30 left in the game.

When the Patriots began the next possession at their own 17-yard line with no time outs remaining, it appeared the game would go to overtime. Instead of sitting on the ball, though, New England began moving downfield with a series of short passes. Then came one big one: Brady's 23-yard strike to Troy Brown to move the ball into St. Louis terri-

tory. After a 16-yard completion to tight end Jermaine Wiggins to the 30-yard line, Brady spiked the ball to stop the clock with seven seconds to go. Vinatieri trotted on and calmly kicked the game-winning, 48-yard field goal as time ran out.

Brady passed for a modest 145 yards, but was named the game's MVP, mostly for the poise he showed on the winning drive. Warner passed for 365 yards for the Rams, who lost despite outgaining the Patriots 427 yards to 267.

■ **_Brady got a Super Bowl hero's welcome at Disney World._**

Super Bowl XXXVII

The Buccaneers, who set records for futility when they first entered the NFL as an expansion team in 1976, ascended to the top of the league in their 27th season by winning the Super Bowl for the first time. The victory came in Jon Gruden's initial year as head coach, and it came against the team Gruden previously had coached.

All season long, Tampa Bay featured a big-play defense that swung momentum to its side. So the Buccaneers followed the same script in the Super Bowl, posting five sacks and intercepting five passes. They turned the game into a rout by returning three of those picks for touchdowns.

Tampa Bay's defense made its presence felt right from the start. After an early turn-over gave the Raiders possession in Buccaneers' territory, defensive end Simeon Rice sacked Oakland quarterback Rich Gannon, and the Raiders had to settle for a field goal and a 3-0 lead. Later in the period, with the score tied 3-3, safety Dexter Jackson picked off Gannon's pass. That led to a go-ahead field goal by Martín Gramatica—and it opened the floodgates. Oakland would not score again until Tampa Bay had built a 34-3 in the third quarter. By then, the outcome was not in doubt. Jackson's interception also was the first of his two in the game. Those thefts would earn him game MVP honors.

Leading 13-3 late in the first half, the Buccaneers put together their two most impressive drives on offense. First, they marched 77 yards to a touchdown on Brad Johnson's five-yard scoring pass to Keenan McCardell 30 seconds before intermission. Then, on its first possession of the second half, Tampa Bay drove 89 yards and took nearly eight minutes off the clock. Johnson and McCardell teamed on an eight-yard scoring pass to cap that drive and make it 27-3. Two plays after that, cornerback Dwight Smith intercepted a pass and returned it 44 yards for another touchdown.

Oakland didn't quit, and capitalized on some Buccaneers' mistakes—like a blocked punt and a fumbled field-goal snap—to pull within 34-21. But any hopes the Raiders had

TAMPA BAY BUCCANEERS 48, OAKLAND RAIDERS 21

January 26, 2003

**Qualcomm Stadium
San Diego, California**

ATTENDANCE: 67,603

Oakland (AFC)	3	0	6	12 —	21
Tampa Bay (NFC)	3	17	14	14 —	48

MVP: **Dexter Jackson, S, Tampa Bay**

HEAD COACHES
TAMPA BAY: **Jon Gruden**
OAKLAND: **Bill Callahan**

■ *Tampa Bay put on a parade for its champs; Brad Johnson and John Lynch enjoyed the ride.*

for a miraculous comeback were dashed when Tampa Bay linebacker Derrick Brooks (44 yards) and Smith again (50 yards) returned interceptions for touchdowns late in the fourth quarter.

Johnson passed for 215 yards and two touchdowns for Tampa Bay, and Michael Pittman added 124 yards on the ground. Gannon passed for 272 yards and two touchdowns for Oakland, but suffered the five intercep-

tions. He also got no help from the Raiders' ground game, which generated only 19 yards on 11 carries.

Gruden had coached the Raiders from 1998 to 2001. But the Buccaneers wanted him on their sideline so much that they sent four high draft picks and $8 million to Oakland in a rare trade involving a coach that brought him to Tampa Bay. The price turned out to be worth it.

Super Bowl XXXVIII

The Patriots won their second Super Bowl in three seasons with another exciting victory in the closing seconds. Kicker Adam Vinatieri, who beat the Rams in game XXXVI with a 48-yard field goal as time out, made a 41-yard kick in this one with four seconds remaining.

Vinatieri's winning kick capped a wild game in which all the scoring was done in the second and fourth quarters. New England led 14-10 at halftime, then appeared to take command when Antowain Smith ran

NEW ENGLAND PATRIOTS 32, CAROLINA PANTHERS 29

February 1, 2004

Reliant Stadium • Houston, Texas

ATTENDANCE: 71,525

Carolina (NFC)	0	10	0 19	— 29
New England (AFC)	0	14	0 18	— 32

MVP: **Tom Brady, QB, New England**

HEAD COACHES
NEW ENGLAND: **Bill Belichick**
CAROLINA: **John Fox**

■ *Givens gets an A for effort and six points for the Patriots.*

two yards for a touchdown 11 seconds into the fourth quarter. But the Panthers, who were playing in the Super Bowl for the first time in their brief franchise history—they were an expansion franchise in 1995—countered quickly. They needed only 2:10 to pull within 21-16 on DeShaun Foster's 33-yard scoring burst (a two-point conversion attempt failed). The next time Carolina had the ball, quarterback Jake Delhomme and wide receiver Muhsin Muhammad teamed on an 85-yard touchdown pass. It was the longest play from scrimmage in Super Bowl history. The two-point conversion try failed again, but the Panthers led 22-21 with 6:53 to play.

It was New England's turn to answer next, and the Patriots marched 68 yards to the go-ahead touchdown. Quarterback Tom Brady completed passes of 25 and 18 yards to wide receiver David Givens, then found Mike Vrabel for a one-yard touchdown pass with 2:51 to go. Vrabel was a starting linebacker on defense who was lined up at tight end in the short-yardage situation. After Kevin Faulk ran for a two-point conversion, the Patriots had a 29-22 lead.

The advantage lasted less than two minutes. Del-

■ *Football deja vu: It's Vinatieri with another game-winner.*

homme completed a 31-yard pass to veteran receiver Ricky Proehl, then found Proehl again for 12 yards and the tying touchdown with 1:08 to play. Finally, the Patriots had the last chance in the back-and-forth final period. After driving his team from its 40-yard line to the Panthers' 40, Brady completed a 17-yard pass to Deion Branch to set up Vinatieri's decisive kick.

Brady completed 32 of 48 passes for 354 yards and three touchdowns to earn his sec-

ond Super Bowl MVP award. Branch added 143 yards on 10 catches for the Patriots, who amassed 481 total yards (to Carolina's 387).

Delhomme completed just 16 of 33 passes for the Panthers, but they were good for 323 yards and three touchdowns. Muhammad led the Panthers with 140 yards on four catches.

The two teams combined to score 37 points in the fourth period. It was the highest-scoring quarter in Super Bowl history.

Super Bowl XXXIX

For the third time in four seasons, the Patriots won the Super Bowl. And for the third time in four Super Bowls, Adam Vinatieri's fourth-quarter field goal made the difference.

This time, though, Vinatieri's decisive kick wasn't as dramatic as his winning kicks in the final seconds of Super Bowls XXXVI and XXXVIII. His 22-yarder in game XXXIX came midway through the fourth quarter and gave New England a 10-point edge over the Eagles. That enabled the Patriots to withstand a late touchdown by Philadelphia and to hang on for the win.

Quarterback Tom Brady was coolly efficient again for New England. He completed 23 of 33 passes for 236 yards and two touchdowns, and he was not intercepted. The two-time Super Bowl MVP didn't earn game honors in this one, however. Instead, the MVP trophy went to wide receiver Deion Branch, who was on the receiving end of a record-tying 11 of Brady's tosses for 133 yards. Branch didn't catch a touchdown pass, but he had several key receptions on three of the Patriots' scoring drives.

After the Eagles tied the game at 14-14 on quarterback Donovan McNabb's 10-yard touchdown pass to running back Brian Westbrook with 3:35 to play in the third quarter, New England answered with the go-ahead touchdown march. Beginning from their 34-yard line, they drove 66 yards in nine plays, the last a two-yard touch-

■ *A trick play sent this touchdown pass to Pats LB Mike Vrabel.*

down run by Corey Dillon 1:16 into the final period.

Philadelphia failed to make a first down on its next possession. Following a punt, Branch's 19-yard catch positioned Vinatieri for his field goal for a 24-14 advantage.

McNabb drew the Eagles close when he teamed with Greg Lewis on a 30-yard touchdown pass with 1:48 play. Philadelphia had one more possession after that, but had to begin at its four-yard line in the final minute. Safety Rodney Harrison sealed the Eagles' fate with his second interception of the game.

McNabb passed for 357 yards and three touchdowns for Philadelphia, although he also was intercepted three times. Wide receiver Terrell Owens, who missed the NFL playoffs with a broken ankle, returned to catch 9 passes for 122 yards.

The Patriots, who won 14 games during the regular season yet had to go on the road to win at Pittsburgh in the AFC title game, joined the Dallas Cowboys of 1992 through 1995 as the only clubs to win three Super Bowls in a four-season span. Brady became the fourth quarterback to win three Super Bowls as a starter, after Terry Bradshaw (four), Joe Montana, and Troy Aikman. And New England coach Bill Belichick became the fourth coach to win three Super Bowls, after Chuck Noll (four), Bill Walsh, and Joe Gibbs.

■ *Harrison (37) exults after one of his picks.*

NEW ENGLAND PATRIOTS 24, PHILADELPHIA EAGLES 21

February 6, 2005

Alltel Stadium • Jacksonville, Florida

ATTENDANCE: 78,125

New England (AFC) 0   7   7 10 — 24

Philadelphia (NFC) 0   7   7   7 — 21

MVP: **Deion Branch, WR, New England**

HEAD COACHES
NEW ENGLAND: **Bill Belichick**
PHILADELPHIA: **Andy Reid**

Super Bowl XL

After winning four Super Bowls in a six-season span in the 1970s, the Steelers' rallying cry was "One for the Thumb" (meaning one more Super Bowl ring). The veterans from those championship teams never did get that title, but a new generation of Pittsburgh players won the franchise's fifth Super Bowl by beating the Seahawks to cap a memorable ride in the 2005 postseason.

For a while, it looked as if Pittsburgh might not even make the playoffs that year. But the Steelers won their last four regular-season games and earned the AFC's sixth (and last) seed in the postseason. After beating division-champions Cincinnati, Indianapolis, and Denver, they became the first number-six seed ever to reach the Super Bowl.

Against the Seahawks, Pittsburgh spotted Seattle a 3-0 lead in a sluggish first quarter in which the Steelers did not generate a first down. But they bounced back to take a 7-3

■ *MVP Hines Ward streaks toward the end zone for the game-clinching touchdown.*

advantage at halftime when quarterback Ben Roethlisberger inched the ball across the goal line on a one-yard touchdown run 1:55 before the intermission. Then, two plays into the second half, speedy running back Willie Parker burst through the Seahawks' defense on a 75-yard touchdown run that was the longest in Super Bowl history.

Leading 14-3, the Steelers were poised to break the game wide open when they drove to Seattle's seven-yard line the next time they had the ball. But Roethlisberger's pass was intercepted by the Seahawks' Kelly Herndon, who returned the theft 76 yards—another Super Bowl record. Three plays later, Matt Hasselbeck tossed a 16-yard touchdown pass to tight end Jerramy Stevens, and Seattle was back in it.

It was still 14-10 when the Seahawks took over possession at their two-yard line late in the fourth quarter. They marched all the way to Pittsburgh's 27 before Hasselbeck's pass for Darrell Jackson near the goal line was picked off by cornerback Ike Taylor. Four plays after that, wide receiver Antwaan Randle El, a former college quarterback, took a reverse handoff from Parker and tossed a 43-yard touchdown pass to Hines Ward for the game-clinching touchdown with 8:56 to play.

■ Cowher capped a great career with his first title.

Randle El was the first wide receiver ever to throw a touchdown pass in the Super Bowl. Ward, who caught five passes for 123 yards, was named the game's MVP.

Hasselbeck passed for 273 yards, and Shaun Alexander rushed for 95 yards for Seattle, which outgained the winners 396 total yards to 339.

With the victory, the Steelers joined the Dallas Cowboys and the San Francisco 49ers as the only franchises to win the Super Bowl five times.

PITTSBURGH STEELERS 21, SEATTLE SEAHAWKS 10

February 5, 2006
Ford Field • Detroit, Michigan
ATTENDANCE: 68,206

Seattle (NFC)	3	0	7	0	– 10
Pittsburgh (AFC)	0	7	7	7	– 21

MVP: **Hines Ward, WR, Pittsburgh**

HEAD COACHES
PITTSBURGH: **Bill Cowher**
SEATTLE: **Mike Holmgren**

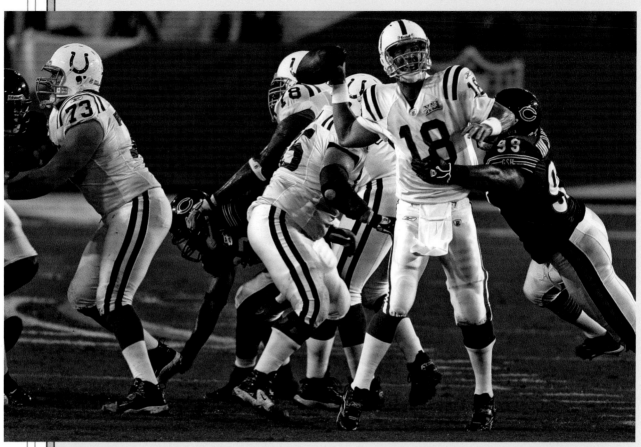

■ *Manning fought off the Chicago rush here and throughout the game to earn MVP honors.*

Super Bowl XLI

For several years, the Colts had fielded excellent teams during the regular season, only to fall short in the playoffs. In 2006, though, they finally put it all together and won the Super Bowl for the first time in 36 years.

Quarterback Peyton Manning completed 25 of 38 passes for 247 yards and a touchdown for the Colts and earned game MVP honors. Running backs Dominic Rhodes (113 yards) and Joseph Addai (77 yards) combined for 190 yards on the ground. Addai, a rookie first-round draft pick in 2006, also caught a game-high 10 passes.

Although they went on to win by a comfortable margin, the game did not begin well for the Colts. Cornerback Devin Hester, a rookie who returned three punts and two kickoffs for touchdowns during the regular season, brought back the opening kickoff 92 yards for a touchdown. Just 14 seconds into the game, the Bears led 7-0.

Chicago still held a 14-9 advantage before Indianapolis went in front for the first time midway through the second quarter. The Colts took over possession at their 42-yard line, and completions from Manning to Marvin Harrison (22 yards) and Dallas Clark (17 yards) quickly moved the ball to the Bears' 19. Five plays later, Rhodes ran one yard for a touchdown and a 16-14 lead 6:09 before halftime.

It stayed that way until the Colts took the second-half kickoff and ate up more than half of the third quarter on a 13-play, 56-yard march to Adam Vinatieri's 24-yard field goal. Then, with the score 22-17 in the fourth quarter, Indianapolis' defense came up with the game-clinching play. On first down from his own 38-yard line, Bears quarterback Rex Grossman lofted

■ *One of Wayne's two catches was this 53-yard score.*

a deep pass down the right sideline. Colts defensive back Kelvin Hayden intercepted, barely kept his feet inbounds, and raced 56 yards for a touchdown and a 12-point lead with 11:44 to play. The Bears did not threaten to score after that, and only crossed midfield again on the game's final play.

Grossman completed 20 of 28 passes for the Bears, but they were good for just 165 yards. He also was intercepted twice and lost a fumble. Chicago turned the ball over five times in all and was outgained 430 total yards to 265.

For the first time in Super Bowl history, the game featured African-American head coaches—the Colts' Tony Dungy and the Bears' Lovie Smith.

INDIANAPOLIS COLTS 29, CHICAGO BEARS 17

February 4, 2007

Dolphin Stadium • Miami, Florida

ATTENDANCE: 74,512

Indianapolis (AFC)	6	10	6	7	— 29
Chicago (NFC)	14	0	3	0	— 17

MVP: **Peyton Manning, QB, Indianapolis**

HEAD COACHES
INDIANAPOLIS: **Tony Dungy**
CHICAGO: **Lovie Smith**

"Super Bowl Shuffle"

The "Super Bowl Shuffle" was a rap song and video recorded by several Chicago Bears' players during their championship season of 1985. The performers included future Hall of Famers such as running back Walter Payton and linebacker Mike Singletary, as well as quarterback Jim McMahon and defensive end Richard Dent, the eventual Super Bowl XX MVP.

Some Bears' players didn't want to take part in the recording sesssion because they felt the song was too boastful or because they felt it would jinx Chicago's chances of winning the Super Bowl (it was recorded well before the game itself).

But the Bears routed the New England Patriots 46-10 in Super Bowl XX to cap a season in which they lost only once in 19 regular-season and postseason games.

At halftime of the Super Bowl, by which time Chicago already led 23-3, the song was played over the Louisiana Superdome's loudspeakers, much to the crowd's

■ *After filming the "Super Bowl Shuffle," the Bears and Mike Ditka shuffled off as champions.*

delight. Among the lyrics of the song was this: "We're not here to start no trouble/We're just here to do the Super Bowl shuffle!"

Swann, Lynn

Lynn Swann was a Hall of Fame wide receiver who played for the Steelers from 1974 to 1982. He was a member of each of Pittsburgh's four Super Bowl winners of the 1970s.

Almost every biography of Swann describes the wide receiver's ballet-like moves and the grace which he brought to his position. Indeed, Swann was a fluid, athletic player who brought a unique artistry to catching passes. That was most evident in Super Bowl X, when he made an acrobatic, juggling catch of a long pass from quarterback Terry Bradshaw. That grab is one of the most famous in Super Bowl history and helped Swann earn MVP honors in the Steelers' 21-17 victory over the Dallas Cowboys.

Swann caught 336 passes, including 51 for touchdowns, in his nine-year career. He earned all-pro honors three times. He was a member of the Hall of Fame's Class of 2001.

In 2006, Swann entered politics, running for governor of Pennsylvania. Though popular there, he lost the race.

■ *Swann was a graceful, talented Hall of Fame receiver.*

Sweep

A sweep is a running play that is designed for the ball carrier to follow his blockers to the outside of either side of the line of scrimmage. At the snap, guards or tackles pull away from the line and run to one side. The running back then follows them, "sweeping" around the end.

Head coach Vince Lombardi's Green Bay Packers championship teams of the 1960s perfected the "power sweep." On the play, running back Paul Hornung or fullback Jim Taylor would follow several blockers around left end or right end.

■ *No. 37 is making a tackle of No. 81.*

Tackle (action)

The act of a player knocking the ball-carrier to the ground. When the ball is snapped and handed to a player, the 11 players on defense attempt to "tackle" whomever has the ball. They do this by either knocking him down or wrapping their arms around the player to pull him down onto the field. They can also "tackle" a ballcarrier by pushing them out of bounds.

Tackles are not an official NFL statistic, but linebackers are the players who most commonly lead their teams in the category.

continued on page 56

Tagliabue, Paul

On October 26, 1989, Paul Tagliabue was selected to be the seventh commissioner in NFL history, replacing the legendary Pete Rozelle. Tagliabue served until 2006 and oversaw many important changes in the NFL.

Born in 1940, Tagliabue played college basketball at Georgetown. He went to law school and had worked with the NFL as a lawyer for 13 years when he was hired as the commissioner in 1989.

Among all of his accomplishments, Tagliabue's longest-lasting legacy may be the fact 21 stadiums were either restructured or newly built during his 17 years in office. Among his first changes in 1990 was the creation of the bye week, giving each team a week off during the season. Other changes included expansion from 28 teams in the league to 32; a four-year television contract; and the expansion of American Bowl games to Germany and Canada. He also hired two doctors to oversee the programs for steroids and drug abuse.

In 1991, the NFL launched the World League of American Football (later NFL Europa), and two years later, Tagliabue helped sign a new seven-year contract with the league's players. Under Tagliabue, the Carolina Panthers and Jacksonville Jaguars began play in 1995. In 1996, upon the Cleveland Browns moving to Baltimore, Tagliabue decided the Browns would get to keep their name, and that the team would be reinstated in 1999.

In 1998, the NFL signed an enormous, eight-year television deal and added an extension of the labor deal with the players. In 2001, the owners agreed to expand to 32 teams and re-align the divisions. After the terrorists attacks of September 11, 2001, Tagliabue decided to postpone games that weekend, with other sports then quickly following the NFL's lead.

■ *Tagliabue oversaw a huge rise in NFL popularity.*

In 2003, the NFL announced the formation of the NFL Network, a national cable-TV group focusing on the league. In 2004, the agreement with DirecTV was extended, and in 2005 the NFL created "Hurricane Katrina Weekend," in which $21 million was contributed to aid the Gulf Coast region.

As part of the globalization of the NFL, in 2005 a regular-season game was played in Monterrey, Mexico. In the spring of 2006 the labor contract with the players' was extended once again.

Tagliabue's biggest regret was allowing both the Rams and Raiders to leave Los Angeles after the 1995 season (to St. Louis and Oakland, respectively), then not getting an NFL team back into the nation's second-largest city over his last 11 years as commissioner. Through 2006, Los Angeles still did not have an NFL team.

In March 2006, Tagliabue announced he would be stepping down, and on September 1, 2006, league executive vice president Roger Goodell took control as NFL commissioner.

At the time of Tagliabue's resignation, the NFL had its highest attendance, a signed labor deal, and a lucrative television contract. Thanks in no small part to him, the NFL was still "the most popular sport in America."

Tampa Bay Buccaneers

Tampa Bay Buccaneers fans have been through the highs and lows when it comes to their NFL team. While the Buccaneers are one of just 17 teams to have won a Super Bowl, they are also the only NFL team ever to lose every game in an entire season.

The city of Tampa was awarded the NFL's 27th franchise in April of 1974. Tampa real estate investor and attorney Hugh Culverhouse eventually took control.

The team's first season was 1976. Even with famed college coach John McKay in charge and with number-one draft pick Lee Roy Selmon, the Buccaneers were not good. The Buccaneers went 0-14 in 1976, and lost their first 12 games of 1977 before winning their last two. The 26 straight losses are still an all-time NFL record—though not one Tampa Bay is proud of.

In 1978, McKay's club opened with a 4-4 record before the Buccaneers faded with injuries. But the winning attitude had been instilled, and in 1979 the Buccaneers remarkably won the NFC Central Division. The club started the season 5-0 and never looked back. Ricky Bell rushed for more than 1,000 yards, and Selmon won the NFL defensive player of the year award.

In the playoffs, the Buccaneers defeated the Philadelphia Eagles 24-17. In the NFC Championship Game, the Buccaneers fell to the Rams 9-0. In 1982, with the help of quarterback Doug Williams, the Buccaneers reached the playoffs for the third time in four seasons. McKay retired after the 1984 season, and Selmon retired in 1985. Selmon's uniform number 63 was retired, the only Buccaneer so honored.

Owner Hugh Culverhouse passed away in 1994, and Malcolm Glazer was given ownership in 1995. In July 1995, Selmon was inducted into the Pro Football Hall of

■ *The orange-clad Bucs struggled in their early years.*

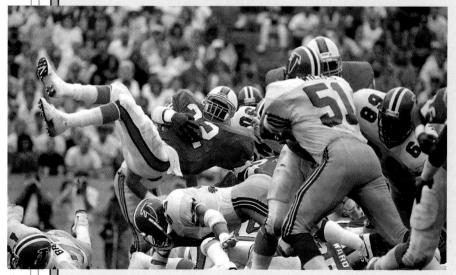

Fame. In October, 1995, the Buccaneers were in first place by themselves for the first time in 14 years. However, the club won just two of its final nine games, and coach Sam Wyche was let go.

The organization began its turnaround in 1996 when Tony Dungy was hired as head coach. The organization's logo and uniform colors were changed in 1997, and the club matched its best season with 10 victories. The Buccaneers won their first postseason game in 18 years, defeating the Lions 20-10.

In 1998, the Buccaneers moved into Raymond James Stadium. In 1999, the club won its first NFC Central title in 18 years but lost 11-6 to the Rams in the NFC Championship Game. Defensive tackle Warren Sapp was named the NFL's defensive player of the year.

The club reached the postseason for the third time in four years in 2000. However, Dungy was relieved of his duties after 2001 despite a franchise-best 56-46 overall record. Jon Gruden was hired from the Raiders as Bucs' new head coach.

The 2002 Buccaneers featured a defense led by defensive end Simeon Rice,

NFL defensive player of the year linebacker Derrick Brooks, and safety John Lynch. They finished 12-4 and then advanced to the Super Bowl for the first time.

In Super Bowl XXXVIII, the Buccaneers' defense returned three interceptions for touchdowns,

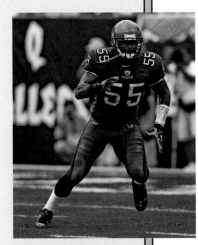

■ **Derrick Brooks gives Tampa Bay veteran leadership.**

including two by Dwight Smith, to defeat the Raiders 48-21. Upon the team's return to Tampa, more than 150,000 fans lined the streets to celebrate during the parade.

Late in 2003, Bruce Allen became the Buccaneers' general manager and, in 2004, wide receiver Michael Clayton caught a club-rookie record seven touchdowns.

In 2005, the Buccaneers posted their third number-one ranked defense in club history (1979, 2002, and 2005), and running back Carnell (Cadillac) Williams was named NFL rookie of the year.

TAMPA BAY BUCCANEERS

CONFERENCE: NFC

DIVISION: SOUTH

**TEAM COLORS:
BUCCANEER RED, PEWTER, BLACK, AND ORANGE**

**STADIUM (CAPACITY):
RAYMOND JAMES STADIUM (65,657)**

**ALL-TIME RECORD:
(THROUGH 2006):
193-304-1**

**NFL CHAMPIONSHIPS
(MOST RECENT):
1 (2002)**

■ *Tackle Larry Allen looks around for someone to block.*

On defense, most teams have either one or two defensive tackles. Aligned in the middle of the defensive line, the defensive tackles first try to slow down the opponents' running game. They can also rush the passer. Defensive tackles are usually the heaviest players on defense. Not normally very quick, they are extremely strong. Some of the best defensive tackles today include Tommie Harris, Jamal Williams, and Kris Jenkins.

Tampa Bay Buccaneers

Please see pages 54-55.

Tackle (position)

Tackle is the only name of a position that can be used for either a player on offense or defense.

On offense, there are two tackles. They line up at either end of the offensive line (left to right, the offensive line would be: left tackle, left guard, center, right guard, right tackle). With a right-handed quarterback, the left tackle is in charge of protecting the quarterback's blind side. For this reason, left tackles are usually the most athletic and best-paid of the five lineman. Today's best tackles are Walter Jones, Jonathan Ogden, Larry Allen, and Willie Anderson.

Tampa Stadium

Tampa Stadium was home of the Tampa Bay Buccaneers from 1976-1997.

The stadium was opened in 1967 when the University of Tampa played Tennessee. The Buccaneers were created in 1974 and the stadium was expanded from 46,700 seats to 72,000 seats. The Buccaneers' first game took place in 1976.

Tampa Bay's best seasons at Tampa Stadium were in 1981 and 1984, when the Buccaneers finished with a 6-2 record. Tampa Stadium had a grass surface. In the stadium's final game, the Buccaneers

Tarkenton, Fran

Fran Tarkenton came off the bench and passed for four touchdowns in his first NFL game. He really didn't slow down the rest of his career.

Tarkenton played 18 seasons, 13 of which were with the Minnesota Vikings (1961-66, 1972-78). He guided the club to three of its four Super Bowls. Though undersized, he not only led the league in passing yards and touchdowns once, but rarely missed a start. In a four-year span from 1973-76, the Vikings had a record of 45-10-1.

Tarkenton was also a tremendous scrambler. Just six feet tall, he would have to scramble out of the pocket to find a passing lane, and he wound up averaging 5.4 yards per carry and rushed for 32 touchdowns during his career. He played five seasons with the New York Giants (1967-1971), passing for 103 touchdowns before being dealt back to the Vikings.

Upon his retirement after the 1978 season, Tarkenton was the NFL's all-time leader in completions (3,686), attempts (6,467), passing yards (47,003), and touchdown passes (342). Only Dan Marino and Brett Favre have surpassed his totals in each of the four categories. Tarkenton was inducted into the Pro Football Hall of Fame in 1986. His uniform number 10 is retired by the Vikings.

■ *Tarkenton is near the top in many career passing stats.*

defeated the Detroit Lions 20-10 in a 1997 NFC Wild Card Game. Tampa Stadium also hosted Super Bowl XVIII (after the 1983 season) and XXV (following the 1990 season). In 1998, the Buccaneers moved

into Raymond James Stadium, which featured a giant, replica pirate ship above the stands behind one end zone.

Taylor, Jim

■ *Taylor was a solid, hard-nosed runner.*

A tough, hard-nosed running back with a crew cut, Jim Taylor was symbolic of the Vince Lombardi-led Green Bay Packers.

Taylor was a second-round draft choice from Louisiana State in 1958. In 1960, he began a string of seven consecutive seasons with at least 200 carries. The Packers won the NFL title in four of those seasons. He posted five consecutive 1,000-yard seasons (1960-64).

Taylor could get the tough yard in short-yardage situations, or he could "run to daylight," meaning he was adept at finding a running lane. His best season was in 1962, when he led the league in rushing and scoring, with a career-high 19 touchdowns. Taylor wound up being selected to five Pro Bowls, and scored at least 10 touchdowns in five consecutive seasons.

Taylor finished his career with one season (1967) with the New Orleans Saints. Upon his retirement, Taylor ranked second to Jim Brown on the all-time NFL list in rushing yards (8,597) and rushing touchdowns (83). Taylor was inducted into the Pro Football Hall of Fame in 1976.

Taylor, Lawrence

Lawrence Taylor was the pre-eminent defensive player of the 1980s and one of the best overall players of all time.

At 6-feet, 3-inches and 241 pounds, Taylor redefined the outside linebacker position with his combination of speed and power. Taylor was athletic enough to cover a receiver running routes, but he specialized in terrorizing quarterbacks with breakneck speed. He was selected to 10 Pro Bowls during his 13-year career.

The second overall pick of the 1981 NFL draft out of North Carolina, Taylor immediately catapulted the Giants into the playoffs his rookie season. He was named the NFL's defensive player of the year a record three times: 1981, 1982, and 1986.

With Taylor as the key defender, the Giants won the Super Bowl twice, in 1986 and 1990. In that first Super Bowl-winning season, Taylor became the only defensive player in the last 35 years to win the NFL's most valuable player award. Taylor led the NFL with 20.5 sacks that season, while dominating games from his outside linebacker position.

■ *Taylor was feared by quarterbacks.*

Upon retirement in 1993, Taylor ranked second in NFL history with 132.5 sacks. His uniform number 56 was retired in 1994 and he was named to the NFL's 75th Anniversary All-Time Team. Though he battled drug problems and off-the-field issues, Taylor was a first-ballot inductee into the Pro Football Hall of Fame in 1999.

Taylor, Jason

Seemingly getting better with age, 32-year-old Jason Taylor was the NFL's defensive player of the year for 2006.

Taylor was a third-round pick out of Akron in 1997, and his five sacks as a rookie were the third-most in club history. Taylor has been a mainstay in the lineup ever since, missing just one game in the last nine seasons. He has the most sacks in

Television (and the NFL)

The NFL is the most popular sport in America, and television has been a big part of the transformation.

The first televised NFL game was on October 22, 1939, when NBC broadcast the Brooklyn Dodgers' 23-14 victory against the Philadelphia Eagles. The game was sent to about 1,000 television sets in the New York City area. In 1950, the Los Angeles Rams became the first team to have all of its games televised, and a year later, in 1951, an NFL game was televised coast-to-coast for the first time as the Rams defeated the Cleveland Browns 24-17 in the 1951 NFL Championship Game.

In 1958, the NFL drew its largest television audience yet, when the Baltimore Colts defeated the New York Giants 23-17 in overtime to win the NFL title. That game is credited with leading to the NFL becoming America's most popular sport. In 1970, ABC began broadcasting Monday Night Football, and in 1980 ESPN began televising the NFL Draft each spring, both of which have only further enhanced America's appreciation of football.

The largest television audience was on February 1, 2004, when 144.4 million viewers watched the Patriots defeat the Panthers in Super Bowl XXXVIII. The highest rated game was Super Bowl XVI, when 49.1 percent of all televisions watched the San Francisco 49ers win.

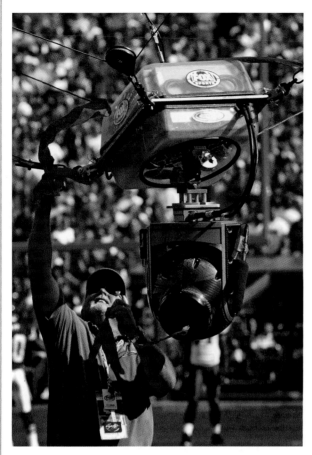

■ *This TV camera swoops above an NFL field.*

the NFL during the 2000s (89.5), and his 106 career sacks are the most in Dolphins' history. Taylor's 18.5 sacks in 2002 are the most in club history.

His seven career touchdowns are the most by a defensive player in club history, and his five fumble recoveries for a touchdown equal the most in NFL history.

In 2006, Taylor registered 13.5 sacks, 10 forced fumbles, and two touchdowns off of turnovers en route to his defensive player of the year honor.

Tennessee Titans

Please see pages 62-63.

Texas Stadium

Texas Stadium hosted its first game in 1971, and is one of the oldest stadiums in the NFL.

Located in Irving, Texas, just outside of Dallas, Texas Stadium has a partial dome. The seats are covered but there is not a roof over the field. This hole over the turf prompted 1970s Cowboys linebacker D.D. Lewis to say the hole in the roof allowed "God to watch His team."

The Cowboys had previously played in the Cotton Bowl. The Cowboys have won 16 of 21 postseason games played in the stadium, and nearly 70 percent of their regular season games. Around the inner rim of the stadium, just above the luxury box section, the Cowboys prominently display the names of people enshrined in their Ring of Honor. The stadium had artificial turf for more than 30 years, until Sportfield Realgrass was installed during the 2002 season.

After 37 seasons in Texas Stadium, the Cowboys are scheduled to move into a new stadium in 2008. Early designs show that the "hole" will return.

T-formation

In 1939 the Chicago Bears, relying on consultant Clark Shaughnessy, unveiled today's version of the T-formation.

The common alignment of the day had five offensive lineman, a quarterback, three running backs, and two receivers. Shaughnessy made two key changes. He had the center directly snap the ball to the quarterback's hands, instead of the one-to-two-yard Shotgun-style snap, and he had the offensive lineman space out approximately one yard apart. These two simple adjustments created more running holes and gave the quarterback more time to focus downfield rather than making sure he had secured the football.

The new alignment paid off in 1940 as the Bears set a then-NFL record by

continued on page 64

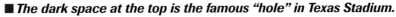

■ *The dark space at the top is the famous "hole" in Texas Stadium.*

Tennessee Titans

The Titans began their existence as the Houston Oilers. On August 3, 1959, the Oilers were one of the eight teams that were part of the newly-formed American Football League (AFL). Owner Bud Adams chose the nickname Oilers. In their first season, 1960, the Oilers defeated the Chargers 24-16 to win the first AFL title. They repeated the feat in 1961. In 1968, the team made a big move, into the famous Astrodome, the first indoor stadium in pro football.

In 1970, the AFL and NFL merged. The Oilers won just one game in 1972 and 1973, but in 1975 the club hired Bum Phillips as head coach and won 10 games. In 1978, the Oilers traded three draft picks and tight end Jimmie Giles to Tampa Bay to get the first pick of the draft. The Oilers selected University of Texas star running back Earl Campbell, who helped the Oilers reach the playoffs each of his first three seasons.

Campbell rushed for more than 5,000

■ *Earl Campbell overwhelmed defenses.*

yards in those first three seasons. He helped the Oilers make it to two straight AFC Championship Games, but they lost both. After an 11-win season in 1980, the Oilers failed to produce a winning record again until 1987. By that time, Warren Moon had been the quarterback since 1984 and Jerry Glanville had become the head coach in 1985. In 1988, the Oilers began a string of six consecutive postseason appearances. With Moon running the exciting Run 'n' Shoot offense, Houston was among the league leaders in scoring.

Two big moves in the mid-1990s were the hiring of head coach Jeff Fisher in 1994

TENNESSEE TITANS

CONFERENCE: AFC

DIVISION: SOUTH

TEAM COLORS:
NAVY, TITANS BLUE, RED, SILVER

STADIUM (CAPACITY):
LP FIELD (68,809)

ALL-TIME RECORD:
(THROUGH 2006):
354-379-6

NFL CHAMPIONSHIPS
(MOST RECENT,
INCLUDES AFL):
2 (1961)

and a move to Tennessee in 1997. The Oilers played the 1997 season at the Liberty Bowl in Memphis. In 1998, the team played at Vanderbilt Stadium in Nashville. In 1999, the Oilers were renamed the Titans, the club's uniforms and colors were changed, and they moved into its new stadium, first called Adelphia Coliseum. With Steve McNair at quarterback and Eddie George at running back, the Titans had a strong, ball-control offense.

The 1999 Titans won 13 games to reach the playoffs. They won a wild-card game with one of the NFL's most memorable plays. The Titans let the Buffalo Bills take a 16-15 lead with 16 seconds left. On the ensuing kickoff, Lorenzo Neal fielded the bouncing kick, handed the ball to Frank Wycheck, who threw a lateral halfway across the field to a wide-open Kevin Dyson, who ran 75 yards down the sideline for a touchdown. The "Music City Miracle" gave the Titans a 22-16 victory. Later, the Titans defeated Jacksonville 33-14 to reach Super Bowl XXXIV.

In Super Bowl XXXIV, the Titans rallied from a 16-0 deficit late in the third quarter to tie the score on Al Del Greco's 43-yard field goal with 2:12 remaining.

But the St. Louis Rams took a 23-16 lead. McNair engineered a 12-play, 87-yard drive capped by a pass to Dyson near the goal line. Rams linebacker Mike Jones tackled Dyson at the 1-yard line as time expired in

one of the most thrilling finishes in Super Bowl history.

In 2002, the Titans won the newly formed AFC South. They reached the AFC Championship Game for the fourth time, but Oakland outlasted the Titans 41-24.

In 2006, the club chose Vince Young with the third overall pick of the draft. At the beginning of the 2007 season, Fisher was enjoying the longest run of any current NFL coach ($12\frac{1}{2}$ seasons).

■ *Vince Young is a bright, young NFL star.*

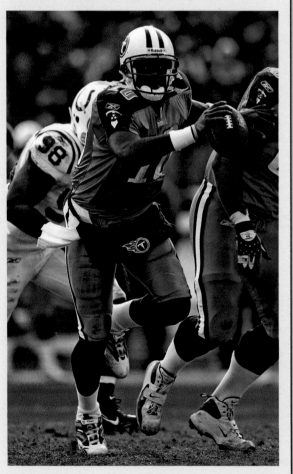

A quartet of Detroit Lions digs into a turkey after Detroit's traditional Thanksgiving Day game.

averaging 29 points per game and won the NFL Championship Game 73-0. Other teams immediately began to copy the new formation. In 1952, the Pittsburgh Steelers became the last team to convert from the Single-Wing to the T-formation. Even today, variations of the T-formation are the basis for most football teams at all levels.

Thanksgiving Day Football

The NFL has been playing Thanksgiving Day football since its inception in 1920, making it part of America's family-holiday tradition.

From 1920-1935, nearly a full schedule of games were played on Thanksgiving Day. There has been at least one game played each year since 1945. As television began to broadcast games, from 1951-1963, the Detroit Lions and Green Bay Packers played against each other on Thanksgiving Day for 13 consecutive years, further enhancing their already fierce rivalry. From 1970-2005, there were two games on Thanksgiving Day, with the Detroit Lions and Dallas Cowboys serving as the hosts each year from 1978-2005. In 2006, the NFL added an evening game to the schedule.

Among the most memorable Thanksgiving Day moments are: in 1929, the Cardinals' Ernie Nevers set an NFL record by scoring 6 touchdowns; in 1993, the Cowboys' Leon Lett attempted to recover a blocked field-goal attempt in the snow,

Thorpe, Jim

In 1950, Jim Thorpe was named the United States' Best Athlete of the First Half-Century. While he played many sports, Thorpe's true legacy is with football.

A Native American from the Sac and Fox Indian tribe, Thorpe's heritage name was Wa-Tho-Huk, meaning "Bright Path," which could explain his impact on the sports world. Thorpe's exploits began in 1908, when he led tiny Carlisle Indian School to an array of impressive victories over the powerhouse colleges of the day. Thorpe gained international fame when he won the pentathlon and decathlon at the 1912 Summer Olympics in Sweden. He also later played major league baseball with three teams (1913-19).

In 1915, Thorpe was signed by the Canton Bulldogs pro football team to the then-immense sum of $250 per game. Thorpe truly was worth the investment, as he could do it all—run with power and speed, boom punts, dropkick with amazing accuracy, and provide bone-jarring tackles on defense. The Bulldogs won unofficial titles in 1916, 1917, and 1919.

When the NFL (then called the American Professional Football Association, or APFA) was founded in 1920, Thorpe was named league president to attract attention from fans. That year, Thorpe was 32 years old and

■ *America's greatest sports legend*

served as more of a gate attraction than star player. Thorpe would perform at halftime—he would stand at the 50-yard line and place-kick a field goal through the upright on one side of the field, then turn around and drop-kick the ball 50 yards through the upright on the other side of the field. He played for seven teams before retiring with the Chicago Cardinals in 1928.

In 1963, Thorpe was one of the very first people inducted into the Pro Football Hall of Fame. One of the main reasons the Hall of Fame is located in Canton, Ohio is because of Thorpe's impact with the Canton Bulldogs in pro football's early days.

■ Three Rivers' Steelers' fans saw four championship teams.

interceptions are the most ever by a Dolphins' linebacker. His seven Pro Bowl appearances are the most ever by a Dolphins' defensive player.

Three Rivers Stadium

Home of the Pittsburgh Steelers from 1970-2000, the Steelers won more than 71 percent of their games at Three Rivers Stadium in 31 years.

The groundbreaking for Three Rivers Stadium was in 1968, and it was ready two years later. The Steelers shared the stadium with baseball's Pittsburgh Pirates. The stadium's name came from its location, where the Monongahela and Allegheny Rivers join to form the Ohio River.

The Steelers, who had never won a postseason game in 37 years prior to moving into Three Rivers Stadium, won four Super Bowls while calling it home. A memorable sight at the stadium was when Pittsburgh's fans, in the 1970s, began waving Terrible Towels, a yellow towel created to spur on the Steelers' defense. The most famous play of Three Rivers Stadium's era was 1972's Immaculate Reception. On the play, which came in the final seconds of the game, the Steelers won their first-ever playoff game on Franco Harris' improbable 60-yard touchdown catch. In 2001, the Steelers moved into Heinz Field.

allowing the Dolphins to kick the game-winning field goal as time expired; and the Lions handing the Packers three of their ten total losses from 1960-63.

Thomas, Zach

Despite being a fifth-round draft choice, Zach Thomas was selected to seven Pro Bowls in his first 11 seasons.

At 5 feet, 11 inches and 228 pounds, Thomas was thought to be too small to play in the NFL. But the Dolphins took a chance on him. In his rookie season of 1996, Thomas became the first rookie to win team MVP honors since famed quarterback Dan Marino 13 years earlier.

Thomas led the Miami Dolphins in tackles in 10 of his first 11 seasons. His four interception returns for a touchdown is a franchise record, and his 17 career

Tiger Stadium

After four seasons at the University of Detroit Stadium, the Detroit Lions began playing at Tiger Stadium (then called Briggs Stadium) in 1938.

The Lions shared the grass-field stadium with baseball's Detroit Tigers from 1938-1974. During the 1950s, Tiger Stadium was the site of two NFL Championship Games. The Lions won both games, defeating the Cleveland Browns 17-16 in 1953 and beating the Browns again, 59-14, in 1957.

In 1961, the stadium was renamed Tiger Stadium. In 1975, the Lions moved into the Pontiac Silverdome, where they remained through 2001. Tiger Stadium remained in use by baseball's Tigers through the 1999 season.

Tight End

Tight ends are tall, strong, and athletic while serving a wide variety of roles on offense.

Lined up next to either offensive tackle, the tight end sometimes serves as a sixth lineman, blocking on running plays. On passing plays, tight ends are athletic enough to get downfield to catch passes.

Most teams use one tight end in most offensive alignments. Sometimes, usually in short-yardage situations, teams employ two or three tight ends. At other times, a team may not have a tight end on the field at all.

The best tight ends of the current era are Antonio Gates and Tony Gonzalez. Among all-time players, Mike Ditka, Ozzie Newsome, and Kellen Winslow are rated among the best in NFL history.

Time of Possession

A statistic that details the amount of time each team is in control of the football throughout the game. There are 60 minutes in a game. When the team has the

■ *Powerful Antonio Gates (right) is the NFL's top tight end.*

■ *QBs like Brett Favre control time of possession.*

ball on offense or is returning a kickoff, it is credited with time of possession.

It is generally accepted that if a team maintains possession for more than 33-34 minutes, they are usually in control of the game. On the flip side, the statistic also shows how long a defense stays on the field, and the longer a defense is on the field, the more it wears down.

Time Out

A time out is when a team stops the clock. Each team is allowed three time outs in each half.

Usually time outs are called late in the half when a team is driving downfield.

Tomlinson, LaDainia

In 2006, LaDainian Tomlinson had one of the finest seasons by a running back—or any player—in NFL history.

Tomlinson scored an NFL record 31 touchdowns to surpass the mark set the previous year by Shaun Alexander. Tomlinson also set a league record with 186 points, breaking the 46-year-mark Paul Hornung set in 1960 with 176 points.

Tomlinson led the league with 1,815 rushing yards, posted nine consecutive 100-yard games, and set a record when he scored 15 touchdowns in a span of five games. He had a record eight consecutive multi-touchdown games.

In six seasons, Tomlinson has essentially rewritten the Chargers' record book. He has established club career records for total touchdowns (111) and rushing yards (9,176), along with many others. By scoring 186 points in 2006, Tomlinson became the first non-kicker since 1945 to outscore another team (the 2006 Raiders had 168 points).

Among his amazing feats, L.T.

➤ Tied a 40-year-old league mark by scoring a touchdown in 18 consecutive games, matching the feat previously set by Lenny Moore.

➤ Scored his 100th career touchdown in 89 games, the fewest ever.

■ Tomlinson set several NFL records in 2006.

➤ Rushed for at least 200 yards in a game four times, equaling the second-most in NFL history.

➤ Rushed for at least 1,200 yards in each of his first six seasons, tying a mark set by Eric Dickerson.

➤ Has 14 career runs of at least 50 yards, third most ever.

Tomlinson can also catch passes. He has had at least 50 receptions each season, highlighted by a club-record 100 catches in 2003. Tomlinson has also passed for 6 touchdowns in his first six seasons. The only non-quarterback in NFL history with more passing touchdowns is Walter Payton, who had 8 touchdown passes.

Through six seasons, Tomlinson is well on his way to becoming one of the greatest running backs of all time. What's surprising is that Tomlinson was not heavily recruited out of high school. He was the MVP of his conference at Waco (Texas) High School, but did not receive many college offers.

Tomlinson chose Texas Christian, where he led the nation in rushing as a junior and senior, including a Division I-A single-game record 406 rushing yards against Texas-El Paso. Texas Christian will not allow anyone to wear his uniform number 5 without Tomlinson's approval, and one day the Chargers will probably be retiring his jersey number 21, too.

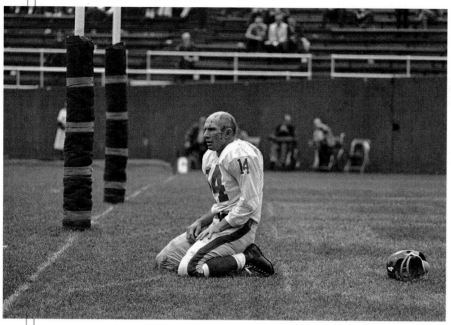

■ *This award-winning photo shows Tittle after he took a big hit.*

Sometimes time outs are called when the 40-second play clock is about to expire and teams do not want to incur a five-yard penalty. The third most common reason time outs are called is on defense, when teams call time out so they can get the ball back with more time remaining on the clock.

Tittle, Y.A.

Some players peak near the end of their career; Yelburton Abraham "Y.A." Tittle certainly was one of them.

Tittle began playing in the All-America Football Conference with the Baltimore Colts in 1948. In 1950, the Colts joined the NFL and Tittle led the league in completions. He joined the 49ers in 1951, and for the rest of the decade Tittle guided San Francisco in solid fashion.

In 1955, he led the league with 17 touchdown passes, and in 1957 the 49ers reached the playoffs while Tittle led the league in completions and completion percentage. Prior to the 1961 season, the New York Giants traded for the 35-year-old quarterback.

For the next three seasons, Tittle led the Giants to the NFL Championship Game. In 1962, he passed for an NFL-leading 33 touchdowns along with 3,224 yards, and his 7 touchdown passes in one game against the Redskins equaled an NFL record. In 1963, at the age of 37, Tittle passed for 36 touchdowns as he won the NFL's most valuable player award. He was the first quarterback to register consecutive 30-touchdown passing seasons, a feat that would be unmatched until Steve Bartkowski and Dan Fouts both accomplished the feat in 1980-81.

Known as "The Bald Eagle" for his lack of hair, Tittle ranked first all-time with 28,339 yards and 212 touchdown passes upon his retirement after the 1964 season. Although he played just four seasons with the Giants, his uniform number 14 was retired by the club in 1965, and Tittle was inducted into the Pro Football Hall of Fame in 1971.

Touchback

A touchback usually occurs when the ball goes through the end zone.

On kickoffs, if the kick returner catches the ball in the end zone and kneels down on one knee, the official immediately blows his whistle, and the play is ruled a touchback. The play is dead and the ball is placed on the 20-yard line. Likewise, if the kickoff bounces or sails out of the end zone, the ball is place on the 20-yard line.

During punts, if the ball bounces out of or sails over the end zone, the whistle is blown and the ball is placed on the 20-yard line.

During play, if the defense recovers a fumble or makes an interception, it can kneel down for a touchback and keep the ball at its own 20-yard-line.

Touchdown

A touchdown (TD) occurs when the ballcarrier breaks the plane of the goal line while maintaining possession of the football. The scoring team is credited with six points. Scoring touchdowns is the goal of every offensive series. When a team scores a touchdown, it sets off a big celebration by the players and the fans rooting for that team. The touchdown is football's most famous and important play.

Touchdowns can be scored in any of the following ways:
- ➤ rushing (running)
- ➤ passing (pass caught in or run into the end zone)
- ➤ kickoff return
- ➤ punt return
- ➤ fumble return
- ➤ fumble recovery
- ➤ interception return
- ➤ blocked punt return
- ➤ blocked field-goal return
- ➤ missed field-goal return

The most touchdowns scored by one

■ *Catching this pass in the end zone earns Chad Johnson a TD.*

■ *The Packers got Brett Favre in a famous trade.*

player in a season is 31 by LaDainian Tomlinson in 2006. The most scored by a team in one game is 11 by the Chicago Bears in the 1940 title game.

Trades

NFL teams can exchange players; these moves are called trades. Trades are not as common in football as they in baseball, for example. A trade can pay off for a team in a big way or it can backfire, as they it gives on a player who later succeeds or at least becomes a big contributor.

The NFL trade with the most players took place in 1989, when the Dallas Cowboys traded Herschel Walker and four draft picks to the Minnesota Vikings for five players and eight draft picks. The 18-player trade helped the Cowboys build their dynasty of the 1990s.

There have also been two 15-player trades (in 1953 and 1971), and in 2000, the New Orleans Saints surprised a lot of people by trading all seven of their draft picks, along with the second-round pick in 2001, to the Washington Redskins in exchange for two draft choices, one of which was used to select Ricky Williams.

Some of the most well-known trades show how things can backfire, when a traded player ends up being a superstar for his new teams. Some examples: In 1992, the Falcons traded second-year quarterback Brett Favre to the Packers for a first-round draft pick; in 1976, the Houston Oilers traded rookie Steve Largent to the Seahawks for an eighth-round draft pick; and in 1987, the Buccaneeers dealt Steve Young to the 49ers for a second-round and fourth-round draft pick.

Tulane Stadium

Tulane Stadium was a college football stadium that served as the home of the New Orleans Saints from 1967 to 1974 and hosted three Super Bowls. It also was known as the Sugar Bowl.

The Kansas City Chiefs upset the Minnesota Vikings 23-7 in Super Bowl IV in January of 1970 at the Sugar Bowl. Two years later, the Dallas Cowboys routed the

Miami Dolphins 24-3 in Super Bowl VI there. In January of 1975, the Pittsburgh Steelers beat the Minnesota Vikings 16-6 in the final Super Bowl played at the site.

Perhaps the most famous moment at the Sugar Bowl came in 1970, when the Saints' Tom Dempsey set an NFL record (since tied) for the longest field goal. He kicked a 63-yarder as time ran out to beat the Detroit Lions.

Tunnell, Emlen

The first African-American, and the first purely defensive player, to be selected to the Pro Football Hall of Fame, Emlen Tunnell was a trailblazer in many ways.

Tunnell attended college at both Toledo and Iowa, interrupted by time with the Coast Guard during World War II. The New York Giants signed him as a free agent in 1948, and he intercepted 17 passes over his first two seasons.

Tunnell returned five interceptions for touchdowns, and his 79 career interceptions rank second all-time to Paul Krause's 81. A gifted open-field runner, he also led the NFL in punt returns twice, and had four punt returns and one kickoff return for a touchdown in his career. He was also regarded as one of the league's toughest tacklers.

After 11 seasons with the Giants, Tunnell joined the Packers in 1959, finishing his final three seasons under famed head coach Vince Lombardi. With Green Bay, Tunnell won his second championship in his final game in 1961.

Tunnell was enshrined in the Pro Football Hall of Fame in 1967, and in 1969 the league selected him as the safety on the NFL's All-Time 50th Anniversary Team.

■ *Tunnell brought an offensive attitude to the defense.*

73

Turner, Bulldog

In the era of players that played both offense and defense, Clyde (Bulldog) Turner was a great center and linebacker for the Chicago Bears.

The Chicago Bears selected Turner in the first round of the 1940 draft. They won four NFL titles during his 13 seasons. Turner played his best in the big games, registering four interceptions in five NFL Championship Games, including a 24-yard interception return for a touchdown in the Bears' record-setting 73-0 romp against the Washington Redskins in the 1940 NFL Championship Game.

■ *Bulldog lived up to his nickname with fierce play.*

Turner was later a head coach for one season, with the New York Titans in 1962, and he posted a 5-9 record. In 1966, Turner was inducted into the Pro Football Hall of Fame. His uniform number has been retired by the Bears.

Two-Minute Drill

Also referred to as a No-Huddle Offense, the Two-Minute Drill is an attempt by the offense to score quickly.

It is usually, but not necessarily, used within the final two minutes of the first half or fourth quarter. By using quick plays and no huddles, a team tries to move a long way quickly. In this alignment, as long as the clock is running, the team does not huddle. If the offense completes a pass, for example, the quarterback, linemen, and rest of the offense sprint to where the football is placed and then snap the ball again without wasting any time.

Some of the NFL's best quarterbacks, such as Tom Brady, Brett Favre, and Joe Montana, would do a tremendous job of completing passes and knowing when to spike the ball to stop the clock. Executing a successful Two-Minute Drill is what usually separates a great quarterback from an average quarterback.

Two-Minute Warning

 With two minutes remaining in the first half, and again with 2:00 left

■ *Eyes on the clock, Patriots QB Tom Brady directs his team during a two-minute drill.*

in the game, the clock is automatically stopped by the officials.

The two-minute warning, while created to before scoreboard clocks told coaches how much time was left, serves as an extra time out for each team.

Two-Point Conversion

After a team scores a touchdown, they usually attempt to kick an extra point. However, sometimes the scoring team will attempt to score two points.

The ball is snapped from the two-yard line, and if the offense can advance the football into the end zone, it is awarded two points. While the two-point conversion has been an active rule in college football for many years, the NFL did not allow two-point conversions until 1994. Since then, the most successful two-point conversions by a team was six by the 1994 Miami Dolphins and 1997 Minnesota VIkings.

In an October 15, 2000, game, the St. Louis Rams' kicker was injured early. Thus, the Rams attempted a two-point conversion after each touchdown, and were successful four times, which is an NFL record for one game.

■ *A powerful, speedy defender, Osi Umenyiora (72) has led the Giants in sacks three times.*

Umbrella Defense

Based on their four consecutive All-America Football Conference titles, the Cleveland Browns were already a powerhouse when they joined the NFL in 1950. How could teams stop quarterback Otto Graham's high-powered offense?

New York Giants coach Steve Owen developed the "Umbrella Defense." The Giants' lined up in the 6-2-2-1 defensive alignment typical for the era (6 defensive lineman, 2 linebackers, 2 cornerbacks, 1 safety). When the ball was snapped, Owen had the two defensive ends and two linebackers retreat from the line of scrimmage at a 45-degree angle, just like the spokes of an umbrella. This zone defense, in which the short, quick passing lanes were cut off, flustered the Browns, and the Giants won four of the first six regular-season games between the clubs.

Variations of the Umbrella Defense are still used to this day, and Owen is in the Pro Football Hall of Fame.

Umenyiora, Osi

Entering his senior season at Troy State, Osi Umenyiora had nine career college sacks, having played three positions (defensive tackle, nose guard, and defensive

Unitas, Johnny

Regarded as one of the greatest quarterbacks of all time, Johnny Unitas was the first NFL star of the TV generation.

Unitas earned instant fame when he was named the most valuable player of the "Greatest Game Ever Played," the 1958 NFL Championship Game. First, he guided the Baltimore Colts to a game-tying field goal at the end of regulation. In overtime, he led them on a touchdown drive that won the game. And he did it all before a national television audience. His actions and that game helped catapult football into becoming America's most popular sport.

It is hard to believe Unitas was playing semipro football three years earlier! The Pittsburgh Steelers had cut him in 1955 after drafting him out of Louisville. He played semipro football one year before the Colts signed him in 1956. Unitas soon became their starter for the next 17 seasons.

From 1956-1960, Unitas completed a touchdown pass in a still-record 47 consecutive games.

Behind Unitas' leadership, the Colts won their second consecutive NFL title in 1959. Unitas was the NFL MVP in 1964 and again in 1967.

Unitas appeared in two Super Bowls, with the Colts losing to the New York Jets in Super Bowl III and defeating the Dallas Cowboys in Super Bowl V. His 75-yard touchdown pass to John Mackey in Super Bowl V ranks as one of the longest pass plays in Super Bowl history. When Unitas retired after playing five games with the San Diego Chargers in 1973, he held NFL records for most passing yards (40,239) and touchdowns (290).

Unitas was named to the Pro Football Hall of Fame in 1979. In 1994, he was one of the four quarterbacks named to the NFL's 75th Anniversary All-Time Team. Unitas passed away in 2002.

■ *Unitas was also famous for his hightop shoes.*

end) in three years. Playing defensive end for the second consecutive year as a senior, Umenyiora excelled. He registered 16 sacks and was a second-round pick by the New York Giants in 2003.

Playing in the shadow of Michael Strahan, Umenyiora had one sack in limited time as a rookie. In 2004, he led the Giants with seven sacks, and in 2005 he not only led the team, but led the NFC with 14.5

■ *Tom Brady in an NFL uniform (without helmet)*

sacks. He had five multiple-sack games, and was named to his first Pro Bowl. In 2006, Umenyiora, despite missing five games because of injury, led the team in sacks for the third consecutive season.

Umpire

One of the seven officials on the football field, the umpire stands directly behind the defensive line. He usually lines up next to the linebackers, about five yards from the line of scrimmage.

Amid the action of 22 players running around him at full speed, the umpire primarily focuses on: watching for false start penalties; holding; making sure offensive linemen do not cross the line of scrimmage; and watching the running backs to ensure they are properly allowed to run their screen-pass routes. On field-goal attempts, the umpire is one of the two officials standing directly underneath either upright.

Uniform

Each of the 32 NFL teams has its own official uniform. While each team may have varying colors and patterns to identify its own brand, each NFL uniform has to follow rules about the size of numerals, length of pants legs, height of socks, etc. Teams have two uniform tops, one dark and one white. During each game, one team wears their white tops and one their darker tops.

In 1970, the NFL made it mandatory for all teams to include the players' last name on their uniform, and in 1973 a standard numbering system was instituted. For example, quarterbacks must have a number between 1-19.

Uniforms created one of the NFL team nicknames: The Cardinals earned their name because their uniforms were "cardinal red."

United States Football League

The United States Football League (USFL) was a spring professional league that lasted three seasons, from 1983 through 1985.

The USFL was founded on the idea that football fans would watch football from February through June, the NFL offseason. Many future NFL stars played in the league, including Doug Flutie, Jim Kelly, Sam Mills, Herschel Walker, Reggie White, and Steve Young.

The league averaged approximately 25,000 fans per game over the course of the three seasons, but teams lost money because of the large contracts handed to keep Walker, Young, and others from signing with the NFL out of college.

■ *USFL teams: Arizona Wranglers (white) and Houston Gamblers.*

The USFL sued the NFL for keeping it from being successful. The USFL won the complicated case, but was awarded only $3 in the spring of 1986. The USFL did not have the financial backing to continue, and the league folded.

Unnecessary Roughness

A general term for an illegal action that results in a 15-yard penalty.

Unnecessary roughness is usually associated with a "late hit," such as when a defender hits an offensive player carrying the ball when that player is out of bounds. Officials also use this term when penalties are thrown for a fight on the field.

If the officials deem that a player used "malicious [very bad] unnecessary roughness" in regards to an incident, the player can be ejected from the game.

Uprights

The uprights are two tall ends of the goal post.

Each upright must be at least 30 feet above the crossbar, or in other words, 40 feet above the field. The height may seem excessive, but it is so the ball does not sail directly over the top of the upright. The most infamous example of this took place

■ *Field goals must go between these two uprights.*

in a 1965 playoff game, when the Green Bay Packers made a controversial field goal (which sailed over the upright) that forced overtime. The next year, the NFL increased the height of the upright to 20 feet above the crossbar, and has since increased it to 30 feet.

A ribbon 4 inches wide by 42 inches long is attached to the top of each upright, allowing the players the opportunity to see the pattern of the wind.

Upshaw, Gene

Needing a big guard to handle the powerful defensive tackles of their rivals, the Oakland Raiders selected 6-foot, 5-inch, 255-pound Gene Upshaw from tiny Texas A&I in the first round of the 1967 draft.

Although tall for his position, Upshaw responded by being the Raiders' starting left guard from 1967-1981, missing just one game. During his 15-year career, the Raiders played in 10 league or conference championship games, and Upshaw's 24 career postseason starts are a club record.

Upshaw has the distinction of being the first player to play in the Super Bowl in three different decades. He was a starter for the Raiders in Super Bowl II (1967 season), XI (1976), and XV (1980), with Oakland winning the latter two games. Upshaw was the team's offensive captain from 1973-1981, and was selected to six Pro

Bowls and one AFL All-Star Game. His 217 games played rank second in Raiders' franchise history.

Upshaw was a first-ballot Pro Football Hall of Fame inductee in 1987, and in 1994 he was named to the NFL's 75th Anniversary All-Time Team. Since 1983, he has served as the director of the NFL Players Association, where he assists in the development and protection of player rights.

Urlacher, Brian

Linebacker Brian Urlacher is one of just five players in NFL history to be named defensive rookie of the year and, seasons later during his career, defensive player of the year.

A phenomenal athlete at the University of New Mexico, where he was an All-America safety as a senior, the Bears selected Urlacher with the ninth overall pick of the first round of the 2000 draft. The Bears decided to let him play middle linebacker, and Urlacher responded by becoming just the second rookie in team history to lead the club in tackles.

Other than in 2004, when Urlacher was limited to nine games because of a ham-

■ *Chicago's Brian Urlacher (54) is one of football's fiercest tacklers.*

string injury, he has been one of the best defensive players in football. He became the first Bears' player since Mike Singletary to lead the team in tackles his first four seasons. Urlacher was named to the Pro Bowl in six of his first seven seasons, and in 2005 he was named the NFL's defensive player of the year.

In his seven seasons, the Bears have reached the playoffs three times and allowed the fewest points in the NFL twice. They ranked third in points allowed in 2006.

Van Brocklin, Norm

In the first game of the 1951 season, quarterback Norm Van Brocklin passed for an amazing 554 yards as the Los Angeles Rams defeated the New York Yanks 54-14. More than 55 years later, that passing yardage total still stands atop the NFL record book as the most ever in a single game.

However, Van Brocklin did not earn a spot in the Pro Football Hall of Fame based on one game. Van Brocklin led the NFL in passing in 1950, 1952, and 1954. An excellent downfield passer, Van Brocklin led the NFL in passing yards per attempt in four of his first six seasons, helping the Rams lead the NFL in scoring three consecutive seasons.

Van Brocklin joined the Rams in 1949. The only problem was that the club already had a great quarterback, Bob Waterfield. The Rams used both quarterbacks for the next four years. In the 1951 NFL Championship Game, Van Brocklin's 73-yard touchdown pass to Tom Fears in the fourth quarter broke a 17-17 tie and led the Rams to the NFL title. Van Brocklin

■ *Van Brocklin was a star passer and coach.*

became the full-time starter in 1953, and kept that job until 1957.

The Eagles traded for Van Brocklin, and by the third season, 1960, the Eagles had defeated the Green Bay Packers to win the NFL Championship Game. With that victory, Van Brocklin owns the distinction of being the only quarterback to ever beat Vince Lombardi in a postseason game.

An excellent athlete, Van Brocklin was also a punter throughout his career. He led the NFL in punting in 1955 and 1956, and had a 42.9-career average.

Van Brocklin retired after winning the NFL title, and promptly became the head coach of the expansion Minnesota Vikings in 1961. Van Brocklin coached a combined 13 seasons for the Vikings (1961-66) and Falcons (1968-1974). He was inducted into the Pro Football Hall of Fame in 1971.

Veterans Stadium

Located in Philadelphia, Veterans Stadium served as home of the Eagles for 31 seasons (1971-2001). Ground was broken in 1967, and, although it was scheduled to open in 1970, poor weather and other delays pushed back the stadium's opening to 1971.

"The Vet" hosted nine playoff games, including the highest-scoring postseason game in NFL history, the Eagles' 58-37 victory over the Detroit Lions in a 1995 NFC Wild Card Game. In 1980, the Eagles

Van Buren, Steve

Life did not begin easily for Steve Van Buren. Born in Honduras, he became an orphan as a child and was sent to New Orleans to live with his grandparents. After playing football at Louisiana State, he became a first-round pick of the Philadelphia Eagles in 1944. The Eagles had never won more than five games in a season in the franchise's 11-year history.

Upon Van Buren's arrival, the Eagles had six straight winning seasons and won two NFL titles. In 1948, he scored the lone touchdown in the snow during the Eagles' 7-0 victory over the Cardinals. The following year, he rushed for a then-championship game-record 196 yards on a muddy field as Philadelphia defeated the Rams 14-0.

Van Buren was the first player to have two 1,000-yard rushing seasons (1947 and 1949). Upon retiring in 1951, Van Buren was the NFL's all-time leader in rushing yards (5,860) and rushing touchdowns (69). He was 1,854 yards ahead of the next player in rushing yards (Tony Canadeo) and had 31 more rushing touchdowns than the next player (Ernie Nevers).

Van Buren led the NFL in rushing in four of his first six seasons. He led the league in rushing touchdowns four times, total touchdowns twice, and kickoff return average twice.

In 1945, Van Buren not only led the NFL in scoring with 110 points, he also outscored the Chicago Cardinals (who had 98 points) and the Pittsburgh Steelers (79 points).

Van Buren was inducted into the Pro Football Hall of Fame in 1965, and in 1994, he was named as one of four running backs on the NFL's 75th Anniversary All-Time Team.

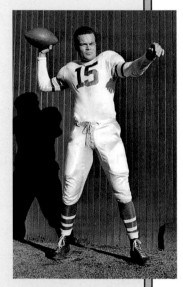

■ *Van Buren was a super-tough runner.*

defeated the Dallas Cowboys 20-7 in the NFC Championship Game to reach Super Bowl XV. In the stadium's final game, the Eagles defeated the Tampa Bay Buccaneers 31-9 in a 2001 NFC Wild Card Game.

In addition to being the Eagles' home, The Vet also hosted the famous annual college game between Army and Navy (17 times), and was the home of baseball's Philadelphia Phillies. The artificial turf, which was in place until 1995, was one of the most unforgiving surfaces in football. The Vet is also remembered for its boisterous fans, who would not only jeer the opposition, but also sometimes boo their own team.

■ *Vick is one of the NFL's most exciting players.*

Vick, Michael

One of the most exciting quarterbacks in NFL history and one of its most multitalented, Michael Vick is one of the league's most popular players.

Vick had a tremendous career at Virginia Tech, where he made one eye-popping play after another and posted a 20-1 record in his two seasons as a starter. The Atlanta Falcons traded up to select Vick with the first overall pick of the 2001 draft.

Vick has posted three of the top five single-season rushing totals for a quarterback in NFL history. In 2006, he became the first quarterback to surpass 1,000 rushing yards in a season, finishing with 1,039. His eight 100-yard rushing games are twice as many as any other quarterback in NFL annals, and his 173 yards at Minnesota in 2002 are the most in a single game by a quarterback. He does all this while also leading his team and passing for numerous touchdowns.

In 2002, Vick guided the Falcons to a 27-7 NFC Wild Card victory at Green Bay. Atlanta became the first visiting team to win a postseason game at Lambeau Field.

Vilma, Jonathan

In college at the University of Miami, Jonathan Vilma led the squad in tackles for three consecutive seasons. Miami was a school that produced great linebackers, and Vilma can now add his name to a list that includes Ray Lewis, Dan Morgan, Mike Barrow, and Darrin Smith.

With the 12th pick of the 2004 draft, the Jets, duly impressed, selected Vilma. With the Jets in 2004, Vilma was named NFL defensive rookie of the year. In 2005, he forced four fumbles while leading the team in tackles. Following the 2005 season, he played in his first Pro Bowl. He led the Jets in tackles again in 2006, as the club made a surprising run to the playoffs.

Vinatieri, Adam

Adam Vinatieri is regarded as the most clutch (meaning "dependable at crucial moments") kicker in NFL history.

In fact, Vinatieri has made so many memorable kicks, it is hard to pinpoint his most important boot. In the 2001 postseason, Vinatieri drilled a 45-yard field goal in the snow to tie the Raiders in a divisional playoff game. Then in overtime, he made the winning 23-yard field goal. A few weeks later, in Super Bowl XXXVI, Vinatieri made a 48-yard field goal as time expired to defeat the St. Louis Rams as the Patriots won their first Super Bowl.

Two seasons later, Vinatieri made a 41-yard field goal with four seconds left as the Patriots defeated the Carolina Panthers 32-29 to win Super Bowl XXXVIII. His fourth-quarter field goal in Super Bowl XXXIX proved to be the difference in the Patriots' dramatic 24-21 win against the Philadelphia Eagles.

Overall, in his 10 seasons with the Patriots, Vinatieri made 18 game-winning field goals in the final minute of regulation or overtime. The Patriots' three Super Bowl championships in four years may never have happened without Vinatieri, whom the club had signed as an undrafted free agent in 1996 out of South Dakota State. In 2006, Vinatieri signed as a free agent with the Colts.

Vince Lombardi Trophy

Presented to the winning team in the Super Bowl, the Vince Lombardi Trophy is the NFL's most coveted award.

The trophy is named in honor of Vince Lombardi, who won Super Bowls I and II as the head coach of the Green Bay Packers. After Lombardi passed away from cancer in 1970, the NFL announced it would rename the Super Bowl trophy the Vince Lombardi Trophy.

The trophy depicts a football on a tall, triangular base. It stands 22 inches, weighs 7 pounds, and is made of sterling silver by Tiffany & Co.

■ *Hines Ward holds the Vince Lombardi Trophy.*

Ward, Hines

Sometimes one game can make a player a hero. Hines Ward, who began his pro career in 1998, was a solid wide receiver for the Steelers. He racked up four 1,000-yard seasons and caught nearly 50 touchdown passes. He made a big mark during in the Steelers' championship season of 2005. He had 11 touchdowns that season. Pittsburgh capped off its great season with a 21-10 victory over Seattle in Super Bowl XL. Ward caught five passes for 123 yards and caught a game-clinching, 43-yard touchdown pass. He was named the game's most valuable player.

Ward has a unique personal background. His father was African-American and his mother Korean. He used his post-Super Bowl fame to help spread football to Korea, visiting there to great acclaim.

Walker, Doak

■ *Walker was an all-around scoring threat.*

Walker was a college superstar, a three-time All-America at SMU, and the 1948 Heisman Trophy winner. After joining the NFL, he continued his success. He was the 1950 rookie of the year and led the league in scoring. In his six years with the Detroit Lions, the team advanced to the NFL Championship Game three times, winning two of them. His long scoring run turned out to be the decisive touchdown in the Lions' 17-7 victory over Cleveland in the 1952 title game.

Walker was not very big (5-11 and 173 pounds), but he was fast and versatile. He did just about everything on offense, from running to receiving to even passing a bit. He also returned kicks and kicked field goals and extra points.

Injuries limited Walker's career to only six seasons. But they were good enough to earn him a spot in the Hall of Fame in 1986.

Walsh, Bill

Few NFL coaches have been as successful or had as lasting and wide-ranging an impact as Bill Walsh. Not only did he revolutionize offensive football in the 1980s, he also influenced a generation of coaches that would follow him.

After a long career as an NFL assistant and college coach, he got his first pro head-coaching job in 1978 with the San Francisco 49ers. The 49ers were 2-14 the year before he took over. Using a new type of attack called the "West Coast" offense, Walsh led the 49ers to three Super Bowl titles (XVI, XIX, and XXIII) in the next 10 years. He was blessed with great players such as quarterback Joe Montana, wide receiver Jerry Rice, and running back Roger Craig. But it was Walsh's genius at crafting a quick-moving, short-pass-based offense that made the 49ers click. Nearly a dozen former Walsh assistant coaches have gone on to become NFL head coaches or coordinators. The West Coast offense was key to many teams' success in the 1990s and early 2000s.

■ *Walsh (center) confers with his greatest QB, Joe Montana (16).*

Walsh retired after the 1988 season and worked as a broadcaster and consultant for pro teams and colleges. He also returned to Stanford, where he coached before joining the 49ers, as head coach from 1992 to 1994. He was inducted into the Pro Football Hall of Fame in 1993.

■ *Kurt Warner had his greatest seasons with the Rams.*

Warfield, Paul

A star wide receiver for two championship teams, Paul Warfield caught 85 touchdown passes in his Hall of Fame career. His average of 20.1 yards per catch is among the best all-time. He played his first six pro seasons with the Cleveland Browns, beginning in 1964. He helped them reach five conference championship games. After being traded to Miami in 1970, he helped that team win Super Bowls VII and VIII. His career numbers (427 catches) are not eye-popping, but his smooth style and big-play attitude helped make him one of the most respected players in NFL history.

Warner, Kurt

Few NFL stories are as unique and surprising as Kurt Warner's. Undrafted after college, Warner held a series of jobs, including bagging groceries, while he tried out for different teams. He caught on with the indoor Arena Football League's Iowa Barnstormers. He led them to an Arena Bowl championship and caught the eye of NFL scouts. After a summer playing for the Amsterdam Admirals in NFL Europe, he was a backup during the 1998 season with the St. Louis Rams. He took over the starting job in 1999 and was named the league MVP after throwing 41 touchdown passes. His power passing led St. Louis to victory in Super Bowl XXXIV, where he was named the game's MVP. In the next two seasons, he continued his amazing run, throwing for more than 8,000 yards in 2000-01.

Warner's rags-to-riches story amazed fans, even those who didn't follow football that often, and he was briefly a national hero. However, Warner suffered some injuries that led to St. Louis letting him go. He played one year with the New York Giants and joined the Arizona Cardinals in 2005. No matter where he plays, however, Warner's stunning rise to success, from grocery story to the Super Bowl, will remain a part of NFL history.

Washington Redskins

Please see pages 90-91.

Wayne, Reggie

Reggie Wayne emerged in 2004 as one of the NFL's top receivers . . . that few people had heard of. Though he played on the powerful Indianapolis Colts' offense, he was overshadowed by superstar Marvin Harrison. In 2004, however, Wayne set a career high with 12 touchdowns, and just kept getting better. In 2006, as the Colts earned their first trip to the Super Bowl since moving to Indy, Wayne set career highs with 1,310 receiving yards and 86 catches. He earned his first selection to the AFC Pro Bowl squad.

Weak Side

In an offensive formation, the tight end is usually one end of the offensive line or the other. The side opposite where the tight end is lined up is called the "weak" side because the offense has one less blocker there.

West Coast Offense

The West Coast Offense has come to mean any offensive strategy that depends on short, high-percentage passes and timing routes between the quarterback and his receivers. In the West Coast Offense, such passes are used for ball control and to set up the run. For many decades,

continued on page 92

Waterfield, Bob

Talk about hot starts. In 1945, Bob Waterfield was the NFL most valuable player and rookie of the year as he led the Cleveland Rams to the championship. A strong-armed passer who excelled at the deep pass, Waterfield helped the Rams (who moved to Los Angeles in 1946) develop one of the league's top offensive attacks. Along with fellow quarterback Norm Van Brocklin, the passing duo led the Rams to three more title games. Waterfield was also an excellent kicker and played defensive back. He was named to the Hall of Fame in 1965.

■ *Waterfield and his wife, actress Jane Russell*

Washington Redskins

The long history of the Washington Redskins includes some of the biggest names in NFL history as well as five NFL championships. The team played its first games in 1932 as the Boston Braves. Owner George Preston Marshall, later inducted as a member of the Hall of Fame, renamed the team the Redskins in 1933 and moved them to Washington D.C. for the 1937 season. Led there by quarterback "Slingin'" Sammy Baugh, another future Hall of Famer, the

Redskins won five division championships in the next eight years. The highlights were their 1937 and 1942 NFL championships. The lowlight was their record 73-0 pasting at the hands of the Chicago Bears in the 1940 title game. They also lost in the title game in 1943 and 1945. Baugh did lead the league in passing, interceptions, and punting in 1943, an unrivaled feat.

After that, it would be more than 25 years before the Redskins approached that level

■ *Star quarterback Sammy Baugh (center) celebrates Washington's 1937 title with teammates.*

of success. Some good players would be on those teams, including quarterback Sonny Jurgensen, halfback Bobby Mitchell, and linebacker Sam Huff, but they didn't even sniff the playoffs. Beginning in 1971, however, new head coach George Allen brought in a crew of veteran players nicknamed the "Over the Hill Gang." They earned playoff spots each year but one from 1971 through 1976, including a berth in Super Bowl VII after the 1972 season. Though they lost that game to Miami, it signaled a comeback for the long-down franchise.

In 1981, Joe Gibbs took over as head coach and led Washington to its greatest run of success ever. The Redskins would play in four Super Bowls in the next 11 seasons, winning three of them. Evidence of Gibbs' ability to win with any players is that three different quarterbacks started Washington's three Super Bowl wins. Joe Theismann came first, using the running of John Riggins to win Super Bowl XVII. The Redskins lost to the Raiders in the following Super Bowl. In 1987, Doug Williams led the team to its next title in Super Bowl XXII. Williams became the first African-American

quarterback to start a Super Bowl. Plus, he was named the game's MVP. Mark Rypien took over for the 1991 team that won Super Bowl XXVI. Other stars of the era included talented receiver Art Monk and defenders such as Dexter Manley and Charles Mann.

■ *Washington's Clinton Portis is an elusive runner.*

The biggest Redskins' news of the past decade occurred in 1999. Businessman Daniel Snyder bought the team and Jack Kent Cooke Stadium for a then-record $800 million. Snyder made headlines as the NFL's youngest owner at age 34, and by becoming very involved in team decisions. All that investment, however, hasn't provided many winners for Washington fans. Since then, a 1999 NFC East Division title is the only bright spot for the 'Skins. Running back Clinton Portis is a recent top player, along with receiver Santana Moss.

WASHINGTON REDSKINS

CONFERENCE: NFC

DIVISION: EAST

TEAM COLORS: BURGUNDY AND GOLD

STADIUM (CAPACITY): FEDEXFIELD (91,704)

ALL-TIME RECORD: (THROUGH 2006): 543–495–27

NFL CHAMPIONSHIPS (MOST RECENT): 5 (1991)

Webster, Mike

■ *Webster's success had a dark ending.*

Webster was the rock-solid center of four Pittsburgh Steelers' Super Bowl championship teams. He didn't miss a game from 1975–1986, a stretch of 150 games. A nine-time Pro Bowl selection, Webster was a great technical blocker and a top-notch leader on a veteran team. In 1988, he joined the Chiefs as a coach, but ended up back in uniform, playing two more years. He retired for good after the 1990 season and was named to the Hall of Fame in 1997.

Sadly, Webster died in 2002 in part, according to doctors, to brain injuries suffered during his long years banging heads in the NFL trenches.

almost every offensive philosophy held the opposite view, relying on the run to control the ball and set up the pass.

Because the West Coast Offense does not refer to a specific system or formation, it is not possible to pinpoint its creator or chief architect. But many football experts credit Bill Walsh, the immensely successful head coach of the San Francisco 49ers from 1979 to 1988, with popularizing it. A majority of NFL teams run their own version of the West Coast Offense today.

Wide Receiver

An offensive position player whose main job is to run downfield and catch passes thrown by the quarterback.

Wide receivers have to be fast, courageous, and deceptive. They must also possess great "hands," that is, the ability to catch any ball thrown their way. An ability to dive or leap well is also an asset, as is a delicate touch when trying to land just inside the out-of-bounds lines after making a catch.

The word "wide" comes from their position at the start of play, 10-20 yards to the right or left along the line of scrimmage from where the center is snapping the ball.

The greatest wide receiver of all time is Jerry Rice, the NFL's all-time leader in touchdowns. Among today's players, top wide receivers include Marvin Harrison, Randy Moss, Steve Smith, Chad Johnson, and Reggie Wayne.

Winning Streaks

A winning streak is when a team wins a large number of games in a row without a loss. The most games won in a row in one season is 14. The 1972 Miami Dolphins first set the mark. They went on to win their playoff games and Super Bowl VII to post the only undefeated season in NFL history. In 2004, the Pittsburgh Steelers won their last 14 games of the regular

White, Reggie

White was as big a personality off the field as he was a supremely talented defensive end on the field. First with Philadelphia and then with Green Bay, he was one of the dominant defensive players of the 1980s and 1990s. Many point to his arrival in Green Bay as a free agent in 1993—he was perhaps the first real superstar to switch teams in that way—as the turning point that led to a Packers' title in Super Bowl XXXI. White is second all-time in sacks with 198. He made 13 Pro Bowls as a defensive end and was named in 1994 to the NFL's 75th Anniversary All-Time Team while still playing—a singular honor. White was a fierce pass rusher, but also outstanding against the run, another rare combination.

White joined the Eagles in 1985 after an All-America career at Tennessee and a year with the USFL. He went to seven straight Pro Bowls with the Eagles and signed a huge contract to join Green Bay. He ended his outstanding career in 2000 after a one-year run with the Carolina Panthers.

Off the field, White was a powerful personality. He was an ordained preacher, leading to his nickname, "The Minister of Defense." He was not at all shy about making his opinions known, and he was respected in and out of football for his strong views on life. Sadly, he died suddenly in 2004 at the age of 43 due to respiratory problems. White was a no-doubt Hall of Fame inductee in 2006.

■ *White's strength made him tough to block.*

season. (They eventually lost in the play-offs.) The longest streak without a loss was by the 1922 Canton Bulldogs; in the span of 25 games, they won 22 and tied three.

The box at right shows the top winning streaks in NFL history.

Winslow, Kellen

Though Kellen Winslow is in the Hall of Fame thanks to a long career as one of the finest tight ends in NFL history, he is an NFL legend for one game. In 1972, the Chargers played the Chiefs in the longest game in NFL history. Going into a second

TOP WINNING STREAKS		
WINS	TEAM	YEAR(S)
21	New England Patriots	2003–04
18	Chicago Bears	1933–34
18	Chicago Bears	1941–42
18	Cleveland Browns	1947–48
18	Miami Dolphins	1972–73
18	San Francisco 49ers	1989–90
18	Denver Broncos	1997–98

overtime period, the teams battled for more than 82 minutes. Winslow made 16 catches and, more importantly, blocked Kansas

■ *Wilson was as tough as he was talented.*

Wilson, Larry

Though he played for mostly unsuccessful St. Louis Cardinals' teams from 1960 to 1972, Larry Wilson was one of the premier defensive players of the decade. Playing free safety in an almost-new way, he was a great pass defender who specialized in interceptions, making 52 in his career. He also perfected the safety blitz, a disruptive move in which the safety suddenly rushes the quarterback at the snap.

Wilson was an extremely tough player, too, rarely missing a game even if he was injured. In fact, he once made an interception with casts on both of his hands to protect broken fingers. He was named to the Hall of Fame in 1978.

City's first try at a winning field goal at the end of regulation. Winslow had to be helped off the field the first time at that point, his body wracked with cramps and bruises. But he went back out for overtime. Finally, the Chargers won 41-38 in the 83rd minute of the game. The photo of a spent Winslow being helped off the field is one of the NFL's most famous. It shows a mighty warrior, who lost 13 pounds during the game, who had given his all, doing whatever he could to try to help his team win.

■ *Action from Wrigley Field during the 1937 NFL Championship Game.*

Knee injuries shortened Winslow's career (1978–1987), but he earned a spot in the Hall of Fame in 1985 for consistent excellence.

World Football League

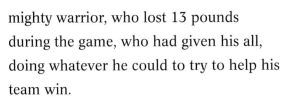
Several pro leagues have been started to challenge the domination of the NFL. The World Football League was one of these. It lasted only two seasons, 1974-75, and had 12 teams at its height. It gained most notice for luring three top Miami Dolphins—Paul Warfield, Larry Csonka, and Jim Kiick—to jump leagues. More than 60 other NFL players of varying levels of stardom went for the quick cash of the WFL. However, though early fan support was good, the league quickly ran out of money. After two seasons (the Birmingham Americans were the only champions), the WFL folded.

Wrigley Field

Only Giants Stadium in New Jersey, home to two NFL teams, has hosted more NFL games than Wrigley Field. The Chicago Bears called the famous field their home from 1921 through 1970. Wrigley also was the home of the Chicago Cardinals from 1931 to 1938. Baseball's Chicago Cubs have played there since 1916.

Wrigley Field is famous for being the last Major League Baseball ballpark to add stadium lighting to allow night games. To the dismay of tradition-loving fans, Wrigley finally got lights in 1988.

Yankee Stadium

This ballpark is famous among baseball fans for the many legends who played there for baseball's Yankees. However, it also has a long football history as well. The New York Giants called Yankee Stadium home from 1956–1973. A short-lived NFL team called the Yankees, starring Red Grange, also played there in 1926–27.

Yankee Stadium was also the site of the 1958 NFL Championship Game between the Colts and Giants, still called "The Greatest Game Ever Played" because of its long-term effect on the popularity of the NFL among fans nationwide.

Yard Line

There are 100 yards in an NFL field but not all of them get yard lines painted on the field. Typically, there is a white yard line every five yards, each stretching from sideline to sideline. Along each sideline are shorter marks indicating each individual yard as well.

The term is also used to indicate field position. "The ball is on the 37-yard line." Or, "the Rams must advance to the 14-yard line for a first down."

Yary, Ron

A durable and talented offensive tackle, Yary helped the Minnesota Vikings reach four Super Bowls. Unfortunately, they lost all of them. It wasn't due to lack of effort or skill on Yary's part. During his 14-year career, he was one of the top O-linemen in the league, earning spots in seven Pro Bowls.

Yary joined the Vikings when they made him the first player overall taken in the NFL Draft in 1968. The team won the NFL championship the following year and began a run that included nine NFC Central titles. Yary missed only two games due to injury in his career. He was named to the Hall of Fame in 2001.

Youngblood, Jack

In the NFL dictionary (if there was one), next to the word "guts," you might see a picture of Jack Youngblood. Already well known for his speed and talent as a pass-rushing defensive end for the Los Angeles Rams, Youngblood became an NFL legend in Super Bowl XIV. After fracturing a bone in his leg in the 1979 divisional playoffs, he didn't leave the lineup. He played in the NFC Championship Game and the Super Bowl with a broken leg! The Rams lost the championship, but Youngblood won the hearts of fans with his gutty performance.

It was nothing new for the seven-time Pro Bowl player, who set a club record by playing in 201 consecutive games (1971–1984). Youngblood's guts and skills were finally recognized in 2001, when he was named to the Hall of Fame.

Young, Steve

Young was the best and most successful left-handed quarterback ever. After emerging from the shadow of being the Joe Montana's backup, Young led the 49ers to a victory in Super Bowl XXIX. He combined great passing skills with sturdy running like few passers before or since.

Young set several passing records at Brigham Young University. He first played in the United States Football League. He joined the NFL's Tampa Bay Buccaneers in 1984 and then moved to the 49ers in 1987. For four seasons, this talented player mostly watched as Joe Montana led the club. In 1991, Young got his chance and won the first of his record-tying six league passing titles. In 1994, in fact, he set a then-record with a passer rating of 112.8. In the Super Bowl after that season, he was the MVP with a record six touchdown passes as the 49ers routed the

■ *Young could do it all—running or passing.*

San Diego Chargers, by a numerically appropriate 49-26 score.

Young was a two-time NFL MVP. Along with six 3,000-yard passing seasons, he also rushed for 43 career touchdowns, most ever by a quarterback. He was inducted into the Hall of Fame in 2005.

Zone

A type of defensive formation in which pass defenders cover an area of the field instead of a specific player. When a receiver enters his zone, the defender then moves to cover that player. Defensive coaches plan different sorts of zones depending on where the ball is on the field and what the score of the game is.

Zone Blitz

A blitz is a play in which defenders other than defensive linemen rush the quarterback. A zone blitz, on the other hand, has one charging lineman dropping back into pass coverage. This can create confusion among the offensive linemen, who are not sure which pass rusher will drop back.

NFL Champions

From the NFL's beginnings in 1920 through 1932, the league's champion was the team with the best regular-season record. There were no playoffs or championship game. From 1933 to 1965, the NFL Championship Game decided the league champ. From 1966 on, the NFL champion was the winner of the Super Bowl.

Year	NFL Champion	Year	NFL Champion
1920	Akron Pros	1946	Chicago Bears
1921	Chicago Staleys	1947	Chicago Cardinals
1922	Canton Bulldogs	1948	Philadelphia Eagles
1923	Canton Bulldogs	1949	Philadelphia Eagles
1924	Cleveland Bulldogs	1950	Cleveland Browns
1925	Chicago Cardinals	1951	Los Angeles Rams
1926	Frankford Yellow Jackets	1952	Detroit Lions
1927	New York Giants	1953	Detroit Lions
1928	Providence Steam Roller	1954	Cleveland Browns
1929	Green Bay Packers	1955	Cleveland Browns
1930	Green Bay Packers	1956	New York Giants
1931	Green Bay Packers	1957	Detroit Lions
1932	Chicago Bears	1958	Baltimore Colts
1933	Chicago Bears	1959	Baltimore Colts
1934	New York Giants	1960	Philadelphia Eagles
1935	Detroit Lions	1961	Green Bay Packers
1936	Green Bay Packers	1962	Green Bay Packers
1937	Washington Redskins	1963	Chicago Bears
1938	New York Giants	1964	Cleveland Browns
1939	Green Bay Packers	1965	Green Bay Packers
1940	Chicago Bears	1966	Green Bay Packers
1941	Chicago Bears	1967	Green Bay Packers
1942	Washington Redskins	1968	New York Jets
1943	Chicago Bears	1969	Kansas City Chiefs
1944	Green Bay Packers	1970	Baltimore Colts
1945	Cleveland Rams	1971	Dallas Cowboys

■ *After filming the "Super Bowl Shuffle," the Bears and Mike Ditka shuffled off as 1985 champions.*

Year	NFL Champion	Year	NFL Champion
1972	Miami Dolphins	1990	New York Giants
1973	Miami Dolphins	1991	Washington Redskins
1974	Pittsburgh Steelers	1992	Dallas Cowboys
1975	Pittsburgh Steelers	1993	Dallas Cowboys
1976	Oakland Raiders	1994	San Francisco 49ers
1977	Dallas Cowboys	1995	Dallas Cowboys
1978	Pittsburgh Steelers	1996	Green Bay Packers
1979	Pittsburgh Steelers	1997	Denver Broncos
1980	Oakland Raiders	1998	Denver Broncos
1981	San Francisco 49ers	1999	St. Louis Rams
1982	Washington Redskins	2000	Baltimore Ravens
1983	Los Angeles Raiders	2001	New England Patriots
1984	San Francisco 49ers	2002	Tampa Bay Buccaneers
1985	Chicago Bears	2003	New England Patriots
1986	New York Giants	2004	New England Patriots
1987	Washington Redskins	2005	Pittsburgh Steelers
1988	San Francisco 49ers	2006	Indianapolis Colts
1989	San Francisco 49ers		

NFL Timeline

1920 At a meeting in Canton, Ohio, a group of amateur and semipro football team owners agree to form the American Professional Football Association, the forerunner of the NFL. Jim Thorpe was named the first president.

1921 The Green Bay Packers joined the association. George Halas took over as sole owners of the Chicago Staleys, later the Bears.

1922 The APFA officially changed its name to the National Football League.

1925 The New York Giants were formed. Red Grange played for the Chicago Bears before a record 75,000 people at an exhibition in Los Angeles.

1929 Ernie Nevers of the Duluth Eskimos sets a still-standing record by scoring 40 points in a single game (six touchdowns and four extra points).

1932 A playoff between two teams–the Chicago Bears and Portsmouth Spartans–tied for the league title is held indoors at Chicago Stadium. The changes in the game due ot the smaller field are so popular they are kept for future seasons. The changes included free forward passing from anywhere behind the line and moving the goalposts to the goal line.

1933 The Eagles join the league. The first NFL Championship Game is played, with the Bears defeating the Giants.

1934 A game between the Giants and Bears on Thanksgiving Day is the first NFL game broadcast on radio.

1936 Jay Berwanger of the University of Chicago is chosen as the first player in the first NFL Draft of college players.

1939 An NFL game was televised for the first time when NBC broadcast the Brooklyn Dodgers-Philadelphia Eagles game from Ebbets Field to the approximately 1,000 sets then in New York

■*Jim Thorpe: America's greatest sports legend*

1940 The Chicago Bears set a still-standing record by defeating the Washington Redskins 73–0 in the NFL Championship Game.

1943 World War II reduced the number of available players. Because of this, several teams stopped playing temporarily. The Pittsburgh Steelers and Philadelphia Eagles actually joined their teams to create the Phil-Pitt Steagles for one year. (The Cardinals and Steelers did the same thing in 1944.) Helmets were made mandatory for all players.

1946 The Cleveland Rams moved to Los Angeles and became the first NFL team west of Chicago. The rival All-America Football Conference was formed; four years later, four of its teams would join the NFL.

1951 The Pro Bowl between the two NFL conference's all-star teams begins regular, annual play. The NFL Championship Game is televised nationwide for the first time.

1958 At Yankee Stadium, the Baltimore Colts defeated the New York Giants 23–17 in sudden-death overtime as the biggest TV audience yet watched. The contest became known as the "Greatest Game Ever Played" because of the impact it had on the league's national popularity.

1960 Pete Rozelle was named commissioner. The former Rams executive would go on to transform the league and make it the nation's most popular. The American Football League (AFL) was formed to challenge the older NFL.

1963 The Pro Football Hall of Fame opens in Canton, Ohio.

1966 The NFL and AFL agree to merge following the 1969 season. They also agreed to have their champions meet in a postseason game beginning after the 1966 season. The NFL's Packers defeated the AFL's Chiefs in what would later become known as Super Bowl I.

1969 The New York Jets become the first AFL team to win a Super Bowl, defeating the Baltimore Colts 16–7 in one of sports' greatest upsets.

1970 Vince Lombardi, who led the Packers to five NFL titles and victories in the first two Super Bowls, died. The Super Bowl championship trophy was then named in his honor. The first Monday Night Football game was played.

1971 Miami defeated Kansas City 27–24 in the longest NFL game ever, an overtime playoff game that lasted 82 minutes, 40 seconds.

1973 Miami wins Super Bowl VII, capping a 17–0 season, the only "perfect" season in NFL history.

1974 The World Football League was formed to challenge the NFL. It would last only two seasons.

1976 The Seattle Seahawks and Tampa Bay Buccaneers joined the NFL as expansion teams. The Cardinals and Chargers played a preseason game in Tokyo, the first NFL game ever played outside North America.

1978 The league raised the number of games played in the regular season to its current total of 16.

1982 Super Bowl XVI received the highest rating (49.0) of any single television show in history, a record it still holds. The regular season that fall was shortened to only nine games due to a labor dispute between players and owners.

1984 Without telling anyone they were moving, the Colts left Baltimore and moved to Indianapolis.

1989 Pete Rozelle retired and Paul Tagliabue was named to replace him as NFL commissioner. The Super Bowl MVP trophy was renamed to honor Rozelle for his many accomplishments. Art Shell of the Raiders became the first African-American head coach in the NFL since Fritz Pollard in 1921.

1991 The NFL formed the World League of American Football, later to be called NFL Europa, to help spread the game to Europe. The league played in summer.

1995 NFL.com became the first pro sports league Web site. The Jacksonville Jaguars and Carolina Panthers joined the NFL as expansion teams.

1999 A new Cleveland Browns team joins the NFL; the old Browns franchise had moved to Baltimore and become the Ravens.

2002 The Houston Texans became the 32nd and most recent member of the NFL. The NFL reorganizes into eight divisions of four teams each.

2004 pats 32-pant 29 The game was witnessed by 144.4 million viewers, making Super Bowl XXXVIII the most-watched program in U.S. television history, February 1.

2005 The Cardinals beat the 49ers 31–14 in Mexico City in the NFL's first-ever regular-season game outside the United States.

2006 Paul Tagliabue retires as NFL commissioner; Roger Goodell takes over.

NFL Top 10s

Here are the top 10 career leaders in some key statistical categories. The records are complete through the 2006 NFL regular season.

Total Touchdowns

Jerry Rice	208
Emmitt Smith	175
Marcus Allen	145
Marshall Faulk	136
Cris Carter	131
Jim Brown	126
Walter Payton	125
Marvin Harrison	122
John Riggins	116
Terrell Owens	116

Touchdown Passes

Dan Marino	420
Brett Favre	414
Fran Tarkenton	342
John Elway	300
Warren Moon	291
Johnny Unitas	290
Peyton Manning	275
Joe Montana	273
Vinny Testaverde	270
Dave Krieg	261

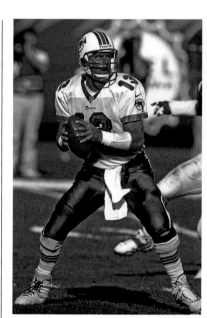

■ *Dan Marino*

Rushing Yards

Emmitt Smith	18,355
Walter Payton	16,726
Barry Sanders	15,269
Curtis Martin	14,101
Jerome Bettis	13,662
Eric Dickerson	13,259
Tony Dorsett	12,739
Jim Brown	12,312
Marshall Faulk	12,279
Marcus Allen	12,243

Receiving Yards

Jerry Rice	22,895
Tim Brown	14,934
James Lofton	14,004
Cris Carter	13,899
Henry Ellard	13,777
Marvin Harrison	13,697
Isaac Bruce	13,376
Andre Reed	13,198
Steve Largent	13,089
Irving Fryar	12,785

■ *Barry Sanders*

Passing Yards

Dan Marino	61,361
Brett Favre	57,500
John Elway	51,475
Warren Moon	49,325
Fran Tarkenton	47,003
Vinny Testaverde	45,281
Drew Bledsoe	44,611
Dan Fouts	43,040
Joe Montana	40,551
Johnny Unitas	40,239

 Brett Favre

Interceptions

Paul Krause	81
Emlen Tunnell	79
Rod Woodson	71
Dick (Night Train) Lane	68
Ken Riley	65
Ronnie Lott	63
Dave Brown	62
Dick LeBeau	62
Emmitt Thomas	58
Mel Blount	57
Bobby Boyd	57
Eugene Robinson	57
Johnny Robinson	57
Everson Walls	57

Sacks

Bruce Smith	200.0
Reggie White	198.0
Kevin Greene	160.0
Chris Doleman	150.5
Richard Dent	137.5
John Randle	137.5
Leslie O'Neal	132.5
Michael Strahan	132.5
Lawrence Taylor	132.5
Rickey Jackson	128.0

Jason Elam

Total Points

Morten Andersen	2,445
Gary Anderson	2,434
George Blanda	2,002
John Carney	1,749
Norm Johnson	1,736
Matt Stover	1,715
Nick Lowery	1,711
Jan Stenerud	1,699
Jason Elam	1,672
Eddie Murray	1,594

Read the index this way: "4:62" means Volume 4, page 62.

Clayton, Michael, **4**:55
Cleveland Browns, **1**:7, 10, 24, 54–55, **4**:53. *See also* Cleveland Browns Stadium
Cleveland Browns Stadium, **1**:49, 55
Cleveland Rams, **3**:22, 54
clipping, **1**:49
clock
    play, **3**:27
    stadium, **3**:10
    stopping the, **3**:80
coach
    assistant, **1**:16–17
    head, **2**:9–10
coffin corner, **1**:49, 52
coin toss, **1**:52
"The Coldest Game". *See* "Ice Bowl"
coldest games, **1**:52, 87, **2**:22, 42
Collins, Kerry, **1**:43, **4**:37
Collinsworth, Cris, **1**:50, **4**:37
Columbus Panhandles, **1**:44
comebacks, greatest, **1**:52, 53
completion, **1**:52
conversion, two-point, **2**:98, **4**:75
Cooper, Earl, **4**:7
cornerback, **1**:53
Coryell, Don, **1**:15, 87, **2**:35, **3**:57
Cosell, Howard, **2**:73
Coughlin, Tom, **2**:32
Cover 2 defense, **1**:56
Cowher, Bill, **1**:56, **2**:10, **3**:28, 47, **4**:26, 47
Craig, Roger, **4**:10, 14, 87
Creekmur, Lou, **1**:56–57
Crennel, Romeo, **1**:55
crossbar, **1**:57
Csonka, Larry, **1**:57, **2**:71, **3**:93, **4**:95
Culpepper, Daunte, **2**:75
Culverhouse, Hugh, **4**:54
Cunningham, Sam, **2**:86
curl, **3**:20
Curtis, Mike, **3**:90

D

Dallas Cowboys. *See also* Texas Stadium
    overview, **1**:58–59
    Ring of Honor, **2**:49, **3**:63, **4**:61
    Super Bowl V, **3**:90
    Super Bowl VI, **3**:91
    Super Bowl X, **3**:95
    Super Bowl XII, **3**:97
    Super Bowl XIII, **4**:4
    Super Bowl XXVII, **4**:20–21
    Super Bowl XXVIII, **4**:22–23
    Super Bowl XXX, **4**:26–27
    Tex Schramm as general manager, **3**:63
    Thanksgiving Day football, **4**:64
Dallas Texans, **1**:12
Davis, Al, **1**:60, **3**:4, 5
Davis, Butch, **1**:55

Davis, Clarence, **3**:96
Davis, Domanick, **2**:17
Davis, Terrell, **1**:65, 73, **4**:30, 31, 32
Davis, Willie, **1**:61, 101
Dawkins, Brian, **3**:25
Dawson, Len, **1**:62, **2**:38, **3**:89
dead ball, **1**:61
Decatur Staleys, **1**:46
deep out, **3**:20
defense
    Cover 2, **1**:56
    Dime, **1**:69, **2**:94
    Doomsday, **1**:70, **2**:96
    Forty-six, **1**:47, 83–84, **2**:6, **3**:73, **4**:11
    Nickel, **2**:94
    No-Name, **2**:96
    Orange Crush, **1**:64, **2**:96, **3**:13, 15, 97
    overview, **1**:61
    Prevent, **3**:34
    Umbrella, **4**:76
defensive back, **1**:61
defensive coordinator, **1**:61–62
defensive end, **1**:62
defensive line, **1**:62–63
defensive tackle, **1**:63
delay of game, **1**:63
Del Greco, Al, **4**:35, 63
Delhomme, Jake, **1**:43, **4**:42, 43
Del Rio, Jack, **2**:33
Dempsey, Tom, **1**:80, **2**:40, 88, **4**:73
Dent, Richard, **4**:11, 50
Denver Broncos. *See also* Invesco Field at Mile High; Orange Crush defense
    in the AFL, **1**:12
    assistant coaches, **1**:17
    overview, **1**:64–65
    Ring of Fame, **2**:29
    Super Bowl XII, **3**:97
    Super Bowl XXI, **4**:12
    Super Bowl XXII, **4**:13
    Super Bowl XXIV, **4**:15
    Super Bowl XXXII, **4**:30–31
    Super Bowl XXXIII, **4**:32–33
    winning streak, **4**:94
Detroit Lions, **1**:66–67, **4**:64. *See also* Ford Field; Pontiac Silverdome; Tiger Stadium
Dickerson, Eric
    overview, **1**:68–69
    Pro Football Hall of Fame, **1**:69, **2**:31
    rushing yards record, **1**:25, 67, 78, **2**:30, **4**:69
Dilfer, Trent, **4**:37
Dillon, Corey, **1**:69, **4**:44
Dime Defense, **1**:69, **2**:94
Ditka, Mike, **1**:68, **2**:58, **3**:91, **4**:11
Dixon, Ron, **4**:36
Dolphin Stadium, **1**:69, 74, **2**:70, **3**:13, **4**:49
Donovan, Art, **1**:69–70, **2**:25
Doomsday Defense, **1**:70, **2**:96
Doran, Jim, **2**:48
Dorsett, Tony, **1**:71, **2**:73, **3**:97

double coverage, **1**:70
Dowler, Boyd, **3**:86, 87
down, **1**:70
draft, **1**:70
draw, **1**:70
drill, two-minute, **2**:18–19, 100, **4**:74
"The Drive", **1**:64, 70
drop back, **1**:71
drop kick, **1**:71
Duluth Eskimos, **1**:71
Dungy, Tony, **1**:71, **2**:25, **4**:49, 55
Dunn, Warrick, **1**:21
Dwight, Tim, **4**:32
Dyson, Kevin, **2**:56, **4**:34, 63

E

Eason, Tony, **4**:11
Edward Jones Dome, **1**:72, **3**:55
Edwards, Glen, **3**:95
Edwards, Herm, **1**:72, **2**:39
Elam, Jason, **1**:72, 80, **2**:40, **3**:20
"The Electric Company", **2**:96
elephant backfield, **1**:74
Eller, Carl, **2**:75, **3**:37
Elway, John
    "The Drive", **1**:64, 70
    great scrambler, **3**:62
    and Joe Montana, **2**:77
    overview, **1**:73
    role within the Denver Broncos, **1**:64, 65, 70
    Super Bowl XXI, **4**:12
    Super Bowl XXXII, **4**:31
    Super Bowl XXXIII, **1**:65, **4**:32, 33
encroachment, **1**:74
end (position), **1**:62
end lines, **1**:74
end zone, **1**:74–75
Ericsson Stadium, **1**:22
Ervins, Ricky, **4**:18
Esiason, Boomer, **1**:50
Evans, Lee, **1**:37
Ewbank, Weeb, **1**:75, **2**:24, 92, 93, **3**:18, 88
"Expansion Bowl", **3**:66
extra point, **1**:75

F

facemask, **1**:76
fair catch, **1**:76
false start, **1**:76
Fantasy Football, **1**:76–77
Fassel, Jim, **4**:37
Faulk, Kevin, **4**:43
Faulk, Marshall, **1**:77–78, **2**:30, **3**:55
Favre, Brett
    AP NFL MVP Award, **1**:17
    forward pass by, **1**:84
    overview, **1**:77
    records, **4**:57
    role within the Green Bay Packers, **1**:101
    and sack by Michael Strahan, **3**:82

Super Bowl XXXI, **1**:100, 101, **4**:28, 29
Super Bowl XXXII, **4**:30, 31
and time of possession, **4**:69
trade, **4**:72
Fears, Tom, **1**:38, 79, **2**:45, **3**:54, **4**:82
"Fearsome Foursome", **1**:78, **2**:34, 96, **3**:9, 55
FedExField, **1**:78–79, **3**:45, **4**:91
field, the football, **1**:66, 79–80
field goal, **1**:80
field judge, **3**:7
field position, **1**:80–81, **2**:101
Filchock, Frank, **1**:27
first-and-10, **1**:81
first down, **1**:81
Fisher, Jeff, **3**:8, **4**:34, 62, 63
Fitzgerald, Larry, **1**:15, 81
flag (pass route), **3**:20
flag (penalty marker), **3**:8, 22
flag football, **1**:81–82
Flaherty, Ray, **1**:23, **2**:91, **3**:64, 76
flat, **1**:82
Flores, Tom, **4**:6, 9
Floyd, William, **4**:24
Flutie, Doug, **4**:79
"The Foolish Club", **1**:82, **2**:21
football, NFL's official, **1**:82–83
Ford, Henry Clay, **1**:67
Ford, Len, **1**:55
Ford, Pres. Gerald, **2**:81, **3**:31
Ford Field, **1**:67, 83, **3**:32, **4**:47
formation
    I-, **2**:22
    overview, **1**:83
    Shotgun, **2**:44, **3**:69
    Single-Wing, **2**:57
    T-, **2**:57, **3**:39, **4**:61, 64
Fortmann, Dan, **1**:44, 85
Forty-six Defense, **1**:47, 83–84, **2**:6, **3**:73
forward pass, **1**:84–86
Foster, DeShaun, **4**:42
foul, personal, **3**:49, 51
Fouts, Dan, **1**:87, **2**:35, **3**:56, 57, **4**:70
Fox, John, **1**:43, **4**:42
Foxboro Stadium, **1**:86
Frankford Yellow Jackets, **1**:86, 88
free agent, **1**:88
Freeman, Antonio, **4**:29, 31
Freeney, Dwight, **1**:88
Frye, Charlie, **1**:55
fullback, **1**:89, **3**:51
fumble, **1**:89
Fuqua, Frenchy, **2**:23

G

game plan, **1**:90
Gannon, Rich, **4**:40, 41
Gansz, Frank, **2**:39
Garcia, Jeff, **3**:59
Garrett, Mike, **3**:89
Garrison, Walt, **3**:91
Gastineau, Mark, **2**:93, **3**:82
Gates, Antonio, **1**:90, **2**:58, **4**:67

National Football League

NOTE: *The numbers following a team's name indicate the volume and page number where the information can be found. "I:36" means Volume I, page 36.*

American Football Conference

East Division		North Division		South Division		West Division	
Buffalo Bills	I:36	Baltimore Ravens	I:24	Houston Texans	II:16	Denver Broncos	I:64
Miami Dolphins	II:70	Cincinnati Bengals	I:50	Indianapolis Colts	II:24	Kansas City Chiefs	II:38
New England Patriots	II:86	Cleveland Browns	I:54	Jacksonville Jaguars	II:32	Oakland Raiders	III:4
New York Jets	II:92	Pittsburgh Steelers	III:28	Tennessee Titans	IV:62	San Diego Chargers	III:56

National Football Conference

East Division		North Division		South Division		West Division	
Dallas Cowboys	I:58	Chicago Bears	I:46	Atlanta Falcons	I:20	Arizona	I:14
New York Giants	II:90	Detroit Lions	I:66	Carolina Panthers	I:42	St. Louis	III:54
Philadelphia Eagles	III:24	Green Bay Packers	I:100	New Orleans Saints	II:88	San Francisco	III:58
Washington Redskins	IV:90	Minnesota Vikings	II:74	Tampa Bay Buccaneers	IV:54	Seattle	III:66

About the Authors

James Buckley Jr. is the author of more than 60 books for young readers on a wide variety of topics—mostly sports! He has written several books on football, including *Eyewitness Football*, *Eyewitness Super Bowl*, and *America's Greatest Game*. Formerly with *Sports Illustrated* and NFL Publishing, he is now the president of the Shoreline Publishing Group, which produced these volumes.

Jim Gigliotti was a senior editor at NFL Publishing and the editor of the league's national GameDay program. He has written hundreds of articles on football for many magazines and Web sites, as well as several children's books on other sports topics.

Matt Marini was also an editor with NFL Publishing, where he oversaw the *NFL Record & Fact Book* among many other writing and editing duties.

John Wiebusch is one of America's leading experts on pro football. As the vice president and creative director of NFL Publishing, he was the editor of the Super Bowl program for 32 years, and author and/or editor of thousands of articles on all aspects of pro football. John is the author of *Lombardi* as well as dozens of other books, and has edited more than 200 titles. He also wrote a popular NFL history column on AOL. He contributed numerous essays on Hall of Fame personalities in these volumes.